A CURRICULUM
IN RELIGION

Edited by

EDWARD A. FITZPATRICK, Ph.D.

in Coöperation with Several
Groups of Religious Teachers

A Basis for the Development of the
HIGHWAY TO HEAVEN SERIES
of Catechism Textbooks
and the
RELIGION IN LIFE CURRICULUM

ST. AUGUSTINE ACADEMY PRESS
HOMER GLEN, ILLINOIS

Nihil obstat

    H. B. RIES,

        Censor Librorum

Imprimatur

    ✠ SAMUEL A. STRITCH,

        Archiepiscopus Milwauchiensis

July 14, 1931

Reprinted in part from
THE CATHOLIC SCHOOL JOURNAL

This book was originally published in 1931 by The Bruce Publishing Company.
This edition reprinted in 2018 by St. Augustine Academy Press.
ISBN: 978-1-64051-047-0

ACKNOWLEDGMENTS

We are indebted particularly to Father Daniel Cunningham, under whose direction this curriculum was prepared for use in the Chicago archdiocese, for permitting us to make it generally available.

We are grateful, too, to the many teachers in parochial schools whose experience has gone into this curriculum.

It is published to help Catholic children everywhere. It may be used in whole or in part, wherever teachers think it may be helpful. No acknowledgment is necessary, and no permission to use the material is needed.

In Chicago, Holy Communion is made the subject matter of the second grade, and the public life of Christ, the subject matter of the third grade. In this national edition of the curriculum, the public life of Christ is made the subject matter of the second grade, continuing the study of the childhood of Christ which is studied in the first grade. In the first grade, a unit is provided for the preparation for first Communion based on the Encyclical of Pope Pius XI, and a more detailed preparation for solemn Communion is made in the third grade. The difference between the first and third grade makes possible a differentiation of treatment.

Naturally, we should welcome any suggestions which come from any experience with this curriculum. We shall revise it as need is shown or as helpful suggestions are received.

EDWARD A. FITZPATRICK,
Dean, Graduate School,
Marquette University.

CONTENTS

GRADE

PAGE

INTRODUCTION 7

I. THE CHILDHOOD OF CHRIST 13

II. THE PUBLIC LIFE OF CHRIST 22

III. PREPARATION FOR SOLEMN HOLY COM-
MUNION 36

IV. OLD TESTAMENT HISTORY 57

V. CHURCH HISTORY 74

VI. THE MASS 101

VII. CHRISTIAN DOCTRINE 119

VIII. CHRISTIAN DOCTRINE 138

INTRODUCTION

Jesus Christ is Foundation. In St. Paul's statement that "Foundation can no man lay other than that which is already laid which is Christ Jesus," we have the secret of Christian life and consequently of Christian education.

Aim of Christian Education. How is this translated into the aim and purpose of education, which is the basic consideration in curriculum making? What is the aim of Christian education? Christ has Himself defined the objective of the Christian life and its preparation in Christian education as follows:

Life everlasting.

To be saved.

To live for ever.

Not to die.

To have life and have it more abundantly.

In the Epistles the Apostles define the Christian educational aim in identical terms:

Life eternal.

Life in Christ.

Life in grace.

Contrast of Christian Education and Social Education. This is in striking contrast with the actual formulation of contemporary public education. The end of Christian education is in no sense merely social, and it is not concerned primarily with social welfare, social well-being or any merely mundane end, though it will have transforming social results. Wealth, power, prestige, position, notoriety, scholarship, research, culture, civic intelligence, social efficiency, vocational skill are not the purpose of Christian education, are not, in fact, in the vocabulary of Christian terminology. Of these aims, those which are good may be incidental results of the Christian scheme. They are not primary, they are not ends at all. "Seek ye first the Kingdom of God and His justice, and all these things shall be added unto you." "Mortality shall be swallowed up in life."

The Natural and Supernatural. But there is no antithesis between spiritual development, or growth in the supernatural life, and the perfection of the natural. Pope Pius XI in his great Encyclical on the *Christian Education of Youth* says with a fine appreciation of the natural and of the comprehensiveness of human life: "The scope and aim of Christian education as here described, appears to the worldly as an abstraction, or rather a something that cannot be attained without the suppression or dwarfing of the natural faculties, and without a renunciation of the activities of the present life, and hence inimical to social life and temporal prosperity, and contrary to all progress in letters, arts, and sciences, and all the other elements of civilization." He concludes with this point: "The true Christian does not renounce the activities of this life, he does not stunt his natural faculties; but he develops and perfects them, by coördinating them with the supernatural. He thus ennobles what is merely natural in life and secures for it new strength in the material and temporal order, no less than in the spiritual and eternal."

The True Christian. The most recent authoritative formulation of the Christian aim is by Pope Pius XI in the recent Encyclical: "Hence the true Christian, product of Christian education, is the supernatural man who thinks, judges, and acts constantly and consistently in accordance with reason illumined by the supernatural light of the example and teaching of Christ; in other words, to use the current term, the true and finished man of character."

Christian Aim is Clear and Simple. With so clear, single, and unmistakably an aim, there ought to be no uncertainty in Christian education. What is at stake is the ultimate spiritual destiny of each man. There should be certainty, no drifting, no doubt. "He who is not with Me is against Me." We should not get lost among a host of inferior aims, or merely social or civic aims. "Render to Cæsar the things that are Cæsar's and to God the things that are God's."

Need for Organization of Material. There must, however, be organization of available material, and of any new materials that may be discovered. Every instrumentality — faith, knowledge, prayer, worship, the sacraments, the Mass, Bible history, church history, and Christian doctrine —must be integrated in a plan of life that reaches the supernatural plane. There must be plan and development. There must be constant reference to the center. There must be secure building on its foundation.

More Immediate Objectives of Christian Education. The ultimate objective of education must be translated into more immediate objectives before the materials can be concretely organized. Underlying this curriculum are the following more immediate objectives deduced from the fundamental aim:

1. To give the child an intimate and continually expanding knowledge of the life of Christ from the very first grade to the eighth.

2. To see that with increasing knowledge there shall go increasing love.

3. To keep before the children throughout the course the ideal of the full measure of the stature of Christ.

4. To give the child a widening appreciation not merely in his education, but in his life that "Foundation can no man lay other than that which is already laid which is Christ Jesus."

5. To give the child a knowledge of the Old Testament as an anticipation of Christ, the Messiah.

6. To give the child a knowledge of the history of the Church as the development of the Kingdom of God on earth.

7. To teach the child to *pray* the Mass with increasing knowledge and devotion.

8. To give the child a thorough and exact knowledge of Christian doctrine, using religious practices, Bible history, church history, poetry, biography, and art, to enrich the study, to prepare the child for its assimilation, and to make it grow "from more to more."

9. To fill the child's mind with the exact words of the great English religious poems, hymns, sayings of Christ, and significant prayers of the Church.

10. To acquaint the child with the great works of religious art.

11. To make real the child's membership in the Body of Christ, until "Christ be formed in him."

12. To make more intelligent, more devotional, and more regular Catholic practice.

13. To let the light of these young students so shine before men that they may glorify the Father Who is in heaven; to live lives of such evident usefulness and virtue, that it is clear what Catholic principles are when they are alive and at work in the world; i.e., incarnate.

14. To have each student become as Christlike as it is possible for him to be, in his devotion to his Father, in his manner of living, in his forgetfulness of self, in his prayers.

Need to Translate into School and Life Activities. The main problem in the construction of a curriculum is to translate a single, definite, unmistakable aim, and the more immediate objectives which are its corollaries into a series of school and life activities that take into account the present capacity and development of the pupil and lead him on through his own activity in a maximum degree to that highest development of man which we call Christlike, or until in what seems humanly daring language of St. Paul, "not I, but Christ liveth in me." And the language is not so daring after all, for what could the Incarnation mean but just that?

Educational Ideas Underlying Curriculum. The next step in our procedure is to translate the ultimate aim of Christian education and its more immediate objective into a series of architectonic ideas for the actual work of constructing the curriculum. These architectonic ideas we also present in summary form:

1. Christ is the center of all Christian teaching.
2. The course must be progressive and cumulative.

3. Nothing shall be taught, even to achieve a temporary purpose, which shall need to be unlearned.

4. The procedure must be psychological, in accord with the pupil's present interests and capacity, and grow with his changes toward the end or purpose of his training.

5. There shall be in each grade a center relating to Christ which will give unity to all the work of the grade, and achieve progressively the fundamental aim of the curriculum.

6. These main centers of interest in each grade receive in the particular grade their main emphasis, though all preceding grades prepare for this main emphasis and future grades carry applications.

7. Christian doctrine is the logical summary of the entire course.

8. The teaching of religion is more inclusive than the teaching of the Catechism.

9. The curriculum must reveal the effects of Catholic culture in human life within the comprehension of the pupils.

10. What is taught in a particular school will be determined by the abilities, past experiences, present mental achievement, and character of environment of the actual class.

11. The curriculum must grow with experience, and be in a state of continuous remaking.[1]

---

[1]For a fuller statement of the summaries contained in this introduction see *The Catholic School Journal* for October, November, and December, 1930.

RELIGION IN GRADE I

Main Interest: The Childhood of Christ

FOR the tots who are in the first grade, the main objective is to give the child the fullest possible knowledge on this level of the Christ Child. Consequently, the texts of the year should deal definitely with the childhood of Christ. Love of the Christ Child is more important at this stage than any knowledge of doctrine. Interest in the Christ Child is more useful in every way than the memorization of all the answers in the Catechism.

As far as possible, everything in the grade should grow out of the story of the childhood of Christ. If a patron is to be selected for this grade it should obviously be the Christ Child. The idea of the patron might be permitted to wait until Christmastide, and then have the children suggest it.

Outline of Main Topics

In the first semester the child will be learning reading, using secular material. Teachers will give only oral instruction in religion in the first semester. The material should include the stories listed below in oral form, acquainting the pupils with the essential vocabulary with main interest around the birth of Christ, culminating in the celebration of Christmas.

In the second semester the child will read from his text or texts or find in supplementary readers the following stories regarding the childhood of Christ:

1. God, the Creator of Heaven and Earth
2. Angels
3. The Announcement to Zachary
4. The Birth of John
5. The Annunciation to Mary
6. Mary's Visit to Elizabeth
7. (Nativity) Jesus is Born
8. The Shepherds Seek Christ
9. The Wise Men Adore Christ
10. Christ is Brought to the Temple
11. The Flight into Egypt
12. The Return to Nazareth
13. Christ in the Temple
14. The Holy Family

Text: Basal and Supplementary

The Basal Text for the course is Sister Bartholomew's *The Book of the Holy Child* (Bruce). The Supplementary Text designed especially to supplement the foregoing is Berdice Moran's *The Childhood of Christ, Verse for Tiny Tots* (Bruce).

Activities

The following activities will be carried out in connection with the above stories:

Clay modeling — the crib; sheep.

Paper cutting — angel; sheep; doves; dove cage; palm trees; booklet; covers.

Poster making — Christmas star; camels; Nazareth; Bethlehem.

Sand-table construction — The cave at Bethlehem; shepherds on the hillside; village of Nazareth; workshop of Joseph; desert scene.

Story-telling — Oral talks on things God has made; What I saw in heaven; What I saw in the Temple; What was said in the Temple; How Jesus spent His day, etc.

Booklet making — Of angel pictures; of pictures of the childhood of Jesus.

Dramatization — The message of the angel; the arrival of the shepherds.

Written Work — Simple sentences in booklets.

Preparation for Holy Communion

The preparation for Holy Communion undertaken in this grade should conform to the fine wisdom and insight of Pius X in that extraordinary document, the *Decree on Early Communion,* (approved Aug. 8, 1910. See also decree of Dec. 20, 1905). The teaching and preparation should be inspired by the spirit and words of the saintly Pope. The substance of the decree is as follows:

The age for the reception of Holy Communion is "the age of discretion," the age at which the child begins to use its reason, that is, about its seventh year, or later, or even sooner.

The determination of when the child is to receive Holy Communion is in the hands of parents and confessor.

The child must be able to understand "according to its capacity": The truth of the Holy Trinity; the Incarnation of God the Son; the death on the cross for our redemption; God is the rewarder of the good and the punisher of the wicked.

As regards the Blessed Sacrament, it is enough if the child "distinguishes the Eucharistic bread from common and material bread so as to approach the Holy Eucharist with such devotion as befits its age."

All those in charge of children must "take the utmost care that after their First Communion the said children should approach the holy table very often, and, if it be possible, even daily, as Jesus Christ and our Holy Mother Church desire it, and that they do so with such devotion of soul as their age allows."

The attention of pastors and teachers is especially called to the phrase "according to its (child's) capacity," as "befits its age," or as "their age allows." The preparation for Holy Communion is not the final study of the Catechism.

The content for this preparation which will often be undertaken by the pastor himself will be found in Father William R. Kelley's, *First Communion* (Benziger), which is recommended as a text. This work when undertaken in this grade should come in the second semester.

Poems

The following poems should be presented orally by the teacher or read from texts or mimeographed sheets.

  *1. *The Creation*, Berdice Moran,
  *2. *The Creator*, John Keble,
   3. *I Wish I Could See the Bright Angel*,
  *4. *Beautiful Angel*, Anonymous,
   5. *When Little Children*, Anonymous,
  *6. *The Annunciation*, Anonymous,
  *7. *Good Night*, Father Tabb,
  *8. *Out of Bounds*, Father Tabb,
   9. *Christmas*, Anonymous,
  10. *Like One I Know*, Nancy Campbell,
  11. *Christmas Night*, Father Faber,
  12. *Christmas Carol*, Sara Teasdale,

13. *Gifts,* Julia Johnson Davis,
*14. *Gifts,* Christina Rossetti,
*15. *A Little Child at the Crib,* Rev. Wm. Ennis,
*16. *Jesus Answers from the Crib,* Rev. Wm. Ennis,
*17. *A Little Boy's Gift,* Hope Cecil,
*18. *A Song,* Charles L. O'Donnell, C.S.C.,
*19. *The Birds,* Hilaire Belloc,
20. *Our Lord and Our Lady,* Hilaire Belloc,
21. *Little Jesus,* Francis Thompson,
*22. *Nazareth,* William Doyle, S.J.,
*23. *Hide and Seek,* Father Tabb,
*24. *A Mother's Quest,* Hugh Francis Blunt.

The simpler poems should be taken up in the first half of the year orally, by the teacher, and the most difficult ones could be similarly taken up at the end of the year, which will serve as a preparation for the later study. There should be throughout the course continual recurrence to these poems. At least the poems starred should be memorized. All should be memorized if time permits. The children should have as a text for the poems: *Religious Poems for Children* (*Primary Grades*) (Bruce).

Picture Study

The children should know the following pictures, which should be presented in connection with the stories studied. Some should be made a matter of special study:

1. The Guardian Angel — Plockhurst,
2. Guardian Angel — Guercine,
3. Annunciation — Titian,
4. Annunciation — Andrea del Sarto,
5. Annunciation — Bouguereau,
6. Adoration of the Shepherds — Murillo,
7. Arrival of the Shepherds — Lerolle,

8. Adoration of the Magi — Durer,
9. The Presentation — Vittore Carpaccio,
10. Flight into Egypt — Plockhurst,
11. Repose in Egypt — Plockhurst,
12. Repose in Egypt — Van Dyck,
13. Christ in the Temple — Hoffmann.

Aspirations of Brief Prayers

As opportunity offers, the following aspirations or others will be taught. One might be selected and written on the board each month, calling attention to it as opportunity permits. The students might prepare aspirations of their own.

1. Jesus, Mary, Joseph,
2. Jesus, Mary, Joseph, I give You my heart and soul,
3. Hallowed be Thy name,
4. Infant Jesus, bless us,
5. Blessed be God.

Prayers

1. The Hail Mary should be taught in connection with the Annunciation.

2. The Our Father, which many of the children will have heard or know partially, should be taught as the prayer which the Christ Child Himself taught when He became a man.

3. The Angelus might possibly be taught (orally) as a development of the Hail Mary.

4. A simple form of morning prayers.

5. A simple form of evening prayers.

Quotations

The children should learn these quotations in connection with the actual situation in which they were

used. They should be frequently asked, Who said it?
Where? When?

1. "God made heaven and earth."
2. "He hath given His angel charge over thee."
3. "Hail, full of grace! The Lord is with thee."
4. "Blessed art thou among women, and blessed is the fruit of thy womb."
5. "Glory to God in the highest and peace on earth to men of good will."
6. "Fear not, I bring you tidings of great joy."
7. "And falling down they adored Him."
8. "Now, O Lord, Thou dost dismiss Thy servant in peace."
9. "Take the Child and His mother and go into Egypt."
10. "He was subject to them."
11. "And not finding Him, they returned into Jerusalem seeking Him."
12. "He grew in age and wisdom and grace before God and men."
13. "And she shall bring forth a son: and thou shalt call His name Jesus. For He shall save His people from their sins" (Matt. i. 21).
14. "For, this day, is born to you a Savior, Who is Christ the Lord, in the city of David" (Luke ii. 11).

Hymns

Hymns are an important factor in reënforcing the general religious instruction and training, valuable for their own content, and, if properly taught, add an element of joy in religious instruction that is quite important. The child should, at the end of instruction, know the great hymns of the Church. For the first grade there is suggested the following to be sung within the voice range of the children.

1. Dear Angel
2. Beautiful Angel
3. Dear Little One

4. What Lovely Infant
5. Come Gather Here Children
6. Jesus, Teach Me How to Pray
7. Baby Jesus Smiling
8. Mother Mary
9. Mary, Mother of God
10. Why Do Bells for Christmas Ring?
11. Guardian Angel from Heaven so Bright

The Liturgy

The child should begin in the very first grade to be interested in the liturgy. But there is real danger of forcing his interest or loading him with information. A simple beginning could be made by having the child note the color of the vestments the priest wears at the Mass, and make them a basis for a first conception of the ecclesiastical year. Changes may be noted day by day and called to his attention.

Religious Practice

A definite part of the program in every grade is to build up the practice of religion in every grade and have the development cumulative throughout the grades. Wherever teachers see opportunity to build up Catholic practice they should do so. Teachers must not confound the lessons that may be essential and the actual practice in the life of the child. The pupil should understand the importance of interior disposition.

In the assignment to grades the purpose is to provide a specific time to see that the practice is established and understood. In some cases the habit will have been established. The cumulative listing of these practices is to emphasize the fact that they are not taught or established once and you are through with them. The practice must continue to be stimulated until it is "securely rooted in the life of the individual."

There should be emphasized in this grade: (1) morning prayer; (2) evening prayer; (3) regular attendance at Mass on Sundays; (4) attendance at Mass on all holydays of obligation.

Practical Life

The translation of the religious knowledge, practice, and attitudes in the day-to-day life of the child must always be an objective in religious education. The elevation of the actual daily life of the individual to a supernatural plane will come about through the character of the individual's motivation. This must be a matter of development: the child must be taken, however, where he is. The lines of development are indicated, but the more specific content is left for the experimentation of the first year.

1. Do a good turn every day for the love of God.
2. Cultivation of virtuous life.
3. Cultivation of school virtues.
4. Promotion of corporal and spiritual works of mercy.

References

1. Eaton, Mary, *The Little Ones,* B. Herder Co., 1922.
2. Brownson, Josephine Van Dyke, *To the Heart of the Child.*
3. Aurelia, Sister Mary and Kirsch, Rev. Felix M., *Practical Aids for Catholic Teachers* (Benziger).
4. Taggart, Marion Ames, *The Wonder Story* and *The Wonder Gifts.*

RELIGION IN GRADE II

Main Interest: The Public Life of Christ

THE main subject matter of the second grade is the public life of Christ. Reviewing the first thirty years of the life of Christ at the beginning of the year, the child then takes up in detail the public life from the baptism by John to the Ascension.

Outline of Main Topics

The topics to be studied include a simple presentation of the following events:

A. *Public Life to the Passion*
　　1. John the Baptist and the Christ
　　2. The Temptation of Christ
　　3. The First Miracle of Cana
　　4. Other Miracles
　　5. The Twelve Apostles are Chosen
　　6. The Sermon on the Mount
　　7. Some Parables
　　8. The Multiplication of the Loaves
　　9. Second Multiplication of Loaves
　　10. The Transfiguration
　　11. Training the Apostles
　　12. Seventy-Two Disciples
　　13. Mary and Martha
　　14. More Parables

15. Raising of Lazarus
B. *The Suffering Life of our Lord*
   1. Victorious into Jerusalem
   2. Driving Sellers Out of Temple
   3. The Plot
   4. Last Supper and the Eucharist
   5. Gethsemane
   6. Trials
   7. Crucifixion
   8. Death
C. *The Glorified Life of Christ*
   1. Resurrection
   2. Ascension

This completes the *introduction* to the religious education by a fairly detailed presentation of the life of Christ within the comprehension of the child. The emphasis is not on doctrine but on love for the Master. The further development will be to have his "love abound more and more in knowledge."

Quotations

The quotations listed should be learned at the time the facts of Christ's public life are being studied, which gives them significance. The quotations in this grade emphasize the Divinity of Christ, the Son of God. The briefer ones at least should be learned as a result of the repetition of it in the instructions. The list for grade three follows:

"The Father loveth the Son: and He hath given all things into His hand" (John iii. 35).

"I am the Good Shepherd, and I know Mine, and Mine know Me" (John x. 14).

"This is My beloved Son, in Whom I am well pleased" (Matt. iii. 16–17; xvii. 5).

"Jesus saith to them: But Whom do you say that I am? Simon Peter answered and said: Thou art Christ, the Son of the living God" (Matt. xvi. 15–16).

"Jesus saith to him: Thou hast said *it*. Nevertheless I say to you, hereafter you shall see the Son of Man sitting on the right hand of the power of God, and coming in the clouds of heaven.

"Then the high priest rent his garments, saying: He hath blasphemed; what further need have we of witnesses? Behold, now you have heard the blasphemy" (Matt. xxvi. 64–65).

"And I saw, and I gave testimony, that this is the Son of God" (John i. 34).

"For God so loved the world, as to give His only begotten Son; that whosoever believeth in Him, may not perish, but may have life everlasting" (John iii. 16).

"And they that were in the boat came and adored Him, saying: Indeed Thou art the Son of God" (Matt. xiv. 33).

"Nathaniel answered Him, and said: Rabbi, Thou art the Son of God, Thou art the King of Israel" (John i. 49).

"She saith to Him: Yea, Lord, I have believed that Thou art Christ the Son of the living God, Who art come into this world" (John xi. 27).

"The Jews answered Him: We have a law; and according to the law He ought to die, because He made Himself the Son of God" (John xix. 7).

"And Pilate wrote a title also, and he put it upon the cross. And the writing was: JESUS OF NAZARETH, THE KING OF THE JEWS" (John xix. 19).

"And the centurion who stood over against Him, seeing that crying out in this manner He had given up the ghost, said: Indeed this Man was the Son of God" (Mark xv. 39).

"And then shall appear the sign of the Son of Man in heaven: and then shall all tribes of the earth mourn: and they shall see the Son of Man coming in the clouds of heaven with much power and majesty" (Matt. xxiv. 30).

"My Lord and my God" (John xx. 28).

"Blessed are the poor in spirit: for theirs is the kingdom of heaven.

"Blessed are the meek: for they shall possess the land.

"Blessed are they that mourn: for they shall be comforted.

"Blessed are they that hunger and thirst after justice: for they shall have their fill.

"Blessed are the merciful: for they shall obtain mercy.

"Blessed are the clean of heart: for they shall see God.

"Blessed are the peacemakers: for they shall be called the children of God.

"Blessed are they that suffer persecution for justice' sake: for theirs is the kingdom of heaven.

"Blessed are ye when they shall revile you, and persecute you, and speak all that is evil against you, untruly, for My sake" (Matt. v. 3–11).

Activities

For supplementary activities the parables offer opportunities for dramatizations.

The Ten Virgins (Matt. xxv. 1–13).

The Good Samaritan (Luke x. 30–37).

The Marriage of the King's Son (Matt. xxii. 1–14).

The parables offer, too, an opportunity for an elaboration of the parables as an approach to creative writing. This is especially true of the parables relating to the kingdom of heaven and its Head.

Booklets begun in previous grades might be continued, or new booklets might be begun on:

The Passion of Christ (using the "Stations of the Cross"),

The Parables of Christ,

The Miracles of Christ,

The Apostles of Christ,

The Appearances of Christ after the Resurrection.

A doctrinal booklet might be made stating the principal doctrinal points under the heading: "*I believe.*"

The public life of Christ offers opportunity for illustration.

Pictures

The children should know the following pictures, which should be presented in connection with the stories studied. Some should be made a matter of special study:

John the Baptist Preaching in the Wilderness — *Doré*
St. John in the Desert — *Raphael*
Temptation of Jesus — *Cornicelius*
The Temptation — *Hoffmann*
The Miracle of Cana — *Tintoretto*
Marriage at Cana — *Doré*
Christ and the Money Changers — *Hoffmann*
Miraculous Draught of Fishes — *Doré*
Christ, the Consoler — *Plockhurst*
Christ Healing the Sick — *Schonherr*
Sermon on the Mount — *Hoffmann*
Sermon on the Mount — *Bida*
Jesus Preaching to the Multitude — *Doré*
Jesus Stilling the Tempest — *Doré*
Jesus Blessing Little Children — *Plockhurst*
Christ Blessing Little Children — *Hoffmann*
Christ Healing the Blind Man — *Bida*
Christ Healing the Ten Lepers — *Seifert*
Christ Healing the Sick — *Hoffmann*
Christ Raising Jairus' Daughter — *Richter*
Raising the Dead — *Hoffmann*
The Daughter of Jairus — *Hoffmann*
Christ and Widow of Naim — *Verchio*
Christ and the Rich Young Man — *Hoffmann*
The Good Samaritan — *Anonymous*
Divine Shepherd — *Murillo*
Prodigal Son — *Molitor*

Good Shepherd — *Dobson*
The Last Supper — *Zimmerman*
Last Supper — *Gebhardt*
Last Supper — *Da Vinci*
Kiss of Judas — *Geiger*
Christ in Gethsemane — *Hoffmann*
Christ in Gethsemane — *Liska*
Easter — *Thomson*
He is Risen — *Plockhurst*
Easter Morning — *Plockhurst*
To Emmaus — *Hoffmann*
On the Way to Emmaus — *Plockhurst*

Religious Vocabulary

Special care must be taken to see that the child's religious vocabulary is increased in connection particularly with the main topic of the grade, and that the new words are taught as the need develops and in the actual situation. Care should be taken to review words previously learned and to be sure a correct meaning is given to them on the child's own level. The words should grow in connotation as his religious knowledge and experience increases.

Words that will generally be taught in this grade are:

Zachary	kingdom	testament
Gabriel	scribes	priests
synagogue	transfiguration	Pilate
miracle	Cæsar	Barabbas
sermon	prodigal son	thorns
disciple	Peter	crucify
centurion	Zebedee	Golgotha
Pharisees	David	forsaken
Samaritans	money-changers	Mary Magdalene
Satan	commandments	sepulcher
David	Jerusalem	resurrection

parable	marriage	Judea
everlasting	betrayed	Galilee
kiss	Judas	scourged

Each teacher will be required to make up her specific lists for her specific children. No stress need be placed on the spelling of these words at present. They may be left on the board for reference.

Poems

The following poems carry on somewhat the same themes as the second grade, and furnish an excellent opportunity for reviewing the whole list. There should be reviewed especially those poems relating to the public life of Christ. The suggestive list follows:

How Children Should Live, Isaac Watts
A Child's Evening Prayer, Samuel Taylor Coleridge
My Neighbor, Father Tabb
A Child's Thought at Christmas, Mary Jane Carr
The Mother of Christ, Aubrey De Vere
The Helper, Rev. Hugh Francis Blunt
The Lowest Place, Christina G. Rossetti
What Have I, Christina G. Rossetti
The Blessed Virgin Mary, H. W. Longfellow
Speak, Little Voice, Rev. Michael Earls, S.J.
Four Things, Henry Van Dyke
A Useful Lesson, Rev. M. Russell, S.J.
For Right is Right, Since God is God, Father Faber
Our Hearts were Made for Thee, O Lord, St. Augustine
Hours are Golden Links, God's Token, Adelaide A. Procter
A Song, Charles L. O'Donnell, C.S.C.
Different Ways, Mary Dixon Thayer
Blessed Candle, Joseph Kinney Collins
A Prayer to Mary, Father H. G. Hughes
Thoughts, Mary Dixon Thayer
The Very Time, Mary Dixon Thayer

Poplars, Joseph Kinney Collins
Trees, Joyce Kilmer
Sheep and Lambs, Katherine Tynan
Flower and Weed, Elvira S. Miller
Communion, Caroline Giltinan
Like One I Know, Nancy Campbell
The Making of Birds, Katherine Tynan
Nails, Leonard Feeney, S.J.
Holy Innocents, Christina G. Rossetti
The Tempest, James T. Fields
Our Lord and Our Lady, Hilaire Belloc
Come to Jesus, Father Faber
Little Things, Rev. F. W. Faber
After a Visit to the Blessed Sacrament, S. M. St. John
Finding You, Mary Dixon Thayer
Child of Nazareth, Rev. J. B. Tabb
A Child's Wish, Rev. Abram J. Ryan
Thanksgiving, Mary Dixon Thayer
Discontent, Sarah Orne Jewett

Additional poems should be used emphasizing the public life of Christ which is the center of interest in the grade. Children should be encouraged to "learn by heart" as many poems as possible. All should be required to learn some; many of the poems should be left to the student's own taste. The more difficult poems will be read to the class by the teacher; some poems will be read for their general idea without detailed study, and some poems will be studied in detail. Poems dealing with the same subject in earlier grades should be recalled to mind after the first reading of new poems. The poems suggested above, with others, are included in *Religious Poems for Children, Primary Grades,* (Bruce).

Aspirations and Brief Prayers

As opportunity offers, the following aspirations or others will be taught. One might be selected and written on the board each month, calling attention to it as opportunity permits. The students might prepare aspirations of their own.

1. Jesus, my God, I love Thee above all things.
2. My Lord and my God.
3. O sweet Heart of Jesus, I implore, that I may ever love Thee more and more.
4. Lord, have mercy on us (3),
   Christ, have mercy on us (3),
   Lord, have mercy on us (3).
5. Lord, save us, we perish.
6. Jesus, meek and humble of heart, make my heart like unto Thine.
7. Jesus, I adore Thee.
8. Jesus, Mary, and Joseph, I love Thee.
9. Blessed be Jesus Christ, true God and true Man.
10. Blessed be the great Mother of God, Mary most holy.
11. Let us give thanks to the Lord, our God.
12. Lord, Thou knowest that I love Thee.
13. Lord, teach me to pray.

Prayers

As the child develops, the form of prayers he will learn will change. The form of morning prayer will undoubtedly change from the simplest form to the use of the liturgical prayers of the Church. This will be generally the development. There will be, of course, an increase in the number of prayers, so that by the end of the elementary school the student will be acquainted with the principal prayers of the Church.

1. Morning prayers
2. Evening prayers
3. Grace before meals
4. Grace after meals
5. Act of Contrition
6. Act of Faith
7. Act of Hope
8. Act of Charity
9. Stations of the Cross
10. The Gloria

Hymns

Hymns are an important factor in reënforcing the general religious instruction and training, valuable for their own content, and, if properly taught, add an element of joy to religious instruction that is quite important. The child should, at the end of instruction, know the great hymns of the Church. For the third grade there is suggested the following to be sung within the voice range of the children:

1. Jesus, Jesus Come to Me
2. Virgin Dearest Mother Mine
3. Little King so Fair and Sweet
4. The Child's Christmas Hymn
5. The Child at Close of Day
6. Mother, Dear, O Pray for Me
7. When Our Saviour Wished to Prove
8. Immaculate Mother
9. Jesus, Tender Shepherd

10. Oh, Sacrament Blessed
11. Holy God We Praise Thy Name

Liturgy

The children should be able to identify the liturgical vestments of the priest at Mass: amice, alb, cincture, maniple, stole, and chasuble. It would be highly desirable for the child to see the priest actually put on his vestments.

Upon visit of a bishop or archbishop for confirmation or for other reasons, the vestments of the bishop or archbishop should be taught. If such an event should not happen while the children are in this grade, the instruction should be given when it does happen. The appointment of a new bishop or archbishop should be used for this purpose, as well as to teach other facts about the Church.

Useful supplementary material for the study of various aspects of the liturgy will be found in Fr. Dunney's *The Mass* (Macmillan), and Fr. M. S. MacMahon's *Liturgical Catechism* (Gill & Son, Dublin), and in the *St. Andrew's Daily Missal* by Dom Le Febvre, O.S.B. (Lohmann).

Religious Practice

A definite part of the program in every grade is to build up the practice of religion in every grade and have the development cumulative throughout the grades. Wherever teachers see opportunity to build up Catholic practice, they should do so. Teachers must not confound the lessons that may be essential and the actual practice in the life of the child. The pupil should understand the importance of interior disposition.

In the assignment, to grade the purpose is to provide a specific time to see that the practice is established and understood. In some cases the habit will have been established. The cumulative listing of these practices is to emphasize the fact that they are not taught or established once and you are through with them. The practice must continue to be stimulated until it is "securely rooted in the life of the individual."

There should be emphasized in this grade:

1. Morning Prayer
2. Evening Prayer
3. Regular attendance at Mass on Sundays
4. Attendance at Mass on all holydays of obligation
5. Angelus
6. Bowing at the name of Jesus
7. Tipping hat or bowing as one passes church
8. Tipping hat when one meets Priest or Sister or other religious
9. Monthly Communion or more frequently

Practical Life

The translation of the religious knowledge, practice, and attitudes in the day-to-day life of the child must always be an objective in religious education. The elevation of the actual daily life of the individual to a supernatural plane will come about through the character of the individual's motivation. This must be a matter of development; the child must be taken, however, where he is. The lines of development are indicated but the more specific content is left for the experimentation of the first year. A teacher should always take advantage of any actual situation, and should always strive to meet difficulties which her children as a group are confronted with, no matter whether it is included in the course of study or not.

1. Do a good turn every day for the love of God.
    a) Daily examination of conscience at night.
    b) Daily specific review of day's thoughts, words, or deeds.
    c) Weekly complete examination of conscience for confession or as a preparation for spiritual Communion.
    d) Daily expiation for the temporal punishment due to sin.
2. Cultivation of virtuous life.
3. Cultivation of school virtues.
4. Promotion of corporal and spiritual works of mercy.

Special attention is directed to the chapters on "The Christian Rule of Life" and "The Christian Daily Exercise" of the *Catechism of Christian Doctrine* approved by the Cardinal, Archbishops, and Bishops of England and Wales, and directed to be used in all their dioceses.

Christian Doctrine

In this grade, perhaps the main contribution to doctrinal teaching will be the specific content of the articles on the Creed on Jesus Christ, His divinity, the facts of His humanity, the second person of the Blessed Trinity, the Savior and Redeemer of men, and particularly the crucifixion, resurrection, and ascension. Growing out of this will be a fuller statement of the facts of His life leading to the establishment of the sacrament of penance, the promise of the Holy Ghost and the descent of the Holy Ghost on the Apostles; the establishment of the Church and of the new priesthood. The basis for the later discussion of the miracles of Christ and of establishment of the sacraments is laid here.

Basal Text and Supplementary Material

The basal text for this grade will be Sr. Bartholomew's, *The Public Life of Christ*, (Bruce) which gives the material on this level. A valuable supplement will be Berdice Moran's story of the public life in verse, *Verse for Tiny Tots*, (Bruce). These are texts prepared to carry out specifically the content of this course of study. They will be used experimentally the first year as a basis for revision if necessary to meet actual classroom conditions.

Further supplementary material may be found in:

1. The Gospels.
2. Mother Loyola, *Jesus of Nazareth*, (Benziger).
3. Sr. James Stanislaus, *Journeys of Jesus*, (Ginn), Book I, II, III.
4. Mary Eaton, *The Little Ones*, (Herder).
5. Josephine Van Dyke Brownson, *To the Heart of a Child*, (Universal Knowledge Foundation).
6. Rev. A. J. Moss, S.J., *Life of Jesus Christ*.
7. Rev. Hugh Pope, *A Catholic Student's Aids to the Bible*, Vol. 5, (Kenedy), (Revised Ed.), (for texts of same incidents in the different Gospels).
8. Sr. Mary Aurelia and Rev. Felix Kirsch, *Practical Aids for Catholic Teachers*, (Benziger).

RELIGION IN GRADE III

Main Interest: Preparation for Solemn
Holy Communion

THE content of the main part of the course for the third grade centers around the preparations for Holy Communion, or in the case of children who have already made the First Communion, for a better understanding of it, and a more significant spiritual life. The fundamental guide for the teacher of the grade in which the child makes his First Confession and First Communion, and of those subsequently who should stimulate regular reception of the Sacrament, are the two papal decrees on Holy Communion. For purpose of reference the text of the Decree on early Communion (Aug. 8, 1910) as related to the "age of discretion," and "the regulations" are quoted herewith.

"From all this it follows that the age of discretion required for Holy Communion is that at which the child can distinguish the Eucharistic from common and material bread and knows how to approach the altar with proper devotion.

"A perfect knowledge of the articles of faith is, therefore, not necessary. A few elements alone are sufficient. Nor is the full use of reason required, since the beginning of the use of reason, that is, some kind of reason, suffices. Wherefore to put off Communion any longer or to exact a riper age for the reception of the same is a custom that is to be rejected absolutely and the same has been repeatedly condemned by the Holy See. Thus, Pius IX, of happy memory, in the letters of Cardinal Antonelli to the Bishops of France given March 12, 1822, severely condemned the growing custom existing in some dioceses of putting off Holy Communion to a maturer age, and rejected the number of years as fixed by them.

"The S. Congregation of the Council on March 15, 1851, corrected a chapter of the Provincial Council of Rouen in which children under twelve years of age were forbidden to receive Holy Communion. This same Congregation of the Discipline of the Sacraments, acting in a similar manner in a case proposed to it from Strassburg on March 25, 1910, in which it was asked whether children of twelve or fourteen years could be admitted to Holy Communion, answered: 'Boys and girls are to be admitted to Holy Communion when they arrive at the age of discretion or attain the use of reason.'

"After seriously considering all these things, the S. Congregation of the Discipline of the Sacraments, at a general meeting held July 15, 1910, in order that the above-mentioned abuses might be removed and the children of tender years become attached to Jesus, live His life, and obtain assistance against the dangers of corruption, has judged it opportune to lay down the following:

"Norm for Admitting Children to First Holy Communion to be observed everywhere:

"1. The age of discretion required both for Confession and Communion is the time when the child begins to reason, that is about the seventh year, more or less. From this time on the obligation of satisfying the precept of both Confession and Communion begins.

"2. Both for First Confession and First Communion a complete and perfect knowledge of Christian Doctrine is not necessary. The child will, however, be obliged to learn gradually the whole Catechism according to its ability.

"3. The knowledge of Christian Doctrine required in children in order to be properly prepared for First Holy Communion is that they understand according to their capacity those mysteries of Faith which are necessary as a means of salvation, that they be able to distinguish the Eucharist from common and material bread, and also approach the sacred table with the devotion becoming their age.

"4. The obligation of the precept of Confession and Communion which rests upon the child, falls back principally upon those in whose care they are, that is, parents, confessors, teachers, and their pastor. It belongs to the father, however, or to the person taking his place, as also to the confessor, as the Roman Catechism declares, to admit the child to First Holy Communion.

"5. The pastor shall take care to announce and hold a General Communion for Children once or several times a year, and on these occasions they shall admit not only First Communicants but also others who, with the consent of their parents and the confessor, have been admitted to the sacred table before. For both classes some days of instruction and preparation shall precede.

"6. Those who have the care of children should use all diligence so that after First Communion the children shall often approach the holy table, even daily, if possible, as Jesus Christ and Mother Church desire, and that they do it with a devotion becoming their age. They should bear in mind their most important duty, by which they are obliged to have the children present at the public instructions in Catechism; otherwise they must supply this religious instruction in some other way.

"7. The custom of not admitting children to confession, or of not absolving them, is absolutely condemned. Wherefore local Ordinaries will take care that it is entirely abolished, even by using canonical punishments.

"8. It is a most intolerable abuse not to administer Viaticum and Extreme Unction to children who have attained the use of reason, and to bury them according to the manner of infants. The Ordinaries of places shall proceed severely against those who do not abandon this custom."

Outline of Main Topics

The purpose of this grade is to give the children, on their level, the general underlying conceptions of religion, or as the Decree has it: "they understand according to their capacity those mysteries of faith which are necessary as a means of salvation, that they be able to distinguish the Eucharist from common or material bread, and also approach the sacred table with the devotion becoming their age." The continuing instruction provided in this curriculum provides for the development and the knowledge acquired here.

1. God the Creator
2. Adam and Eve
3. The Sin of Adam
4. Man, a Pilgrim — Heaven His Home

5. Keep the Commandments
6. The Ten Commandments
   (1   ) I am the Lord thy God. Thou shalt not have strange gods before Me.
   (2   ) Thou shalt not take the name of the Lord thy God in vain.
   (3   ) Remember thou keep holy the Sabbath-day.
   (4   ) Honor thy father and thy mother.
   (5   ) Thou shalt not kill.
   (6, 9) Thou shalt not commit adultery.
          Thou shalt not covet thy neighbor's wife.
   (7,10) Thou shalt not steal.
          Thou shalt not covet thy neighbor's goods.
   (8   ) Thou shalt not bear false witness against thy neighbor.
7. Examination of Conscience
8. The Idea of Redemption
9. The Messiah
10. The Baptism of Christ and the Trinity
11. The Crucifixion and the Resurrection
12. The Catholic Church
13. The Holy Eucharist
14. What the Priest Does in Mass
15. How Can I Be Saved
16. Baptism
17. Peter and the Power of the Keys
18. The Confession
19. Penance
20. Method of Saying Confession
21. Holy Communion

22. The Sacrament of Confirmation
The subtopics are worked out in the syllabus.

Religious Vocabulary

Special care must be taken to see that the child's religious vocabulary is increased in connection particularly with the main topic of the grade, and that the new words are taught as the need develops and in the actual situation. Care should be taken to review words previously learned and to be sure a correct meaning is given to them on the child's own level. The words should grow in connotation as his religious knowledge and experience increases.

Words that will generally be taught in this grade are:

Blessed	commandment	Communion
Sacrament	holy	forgive
Host	Confirmation	tabernacle
loaves	Eucharist	holydays
covet	elevation	temptation
neighbor	Sunday	obligation
sacrifice		

Each teacher will be required to make up her specific lists for her specific children. No stress need be placed on the spelling of these words at present. They may be left on the board for reference.

Quotations

In this grade the quotations center around the sacrifice on Calvary, the Eucharist, and Confirmation. These are all to emphasize Christ's relation to the individual and the individual's love for Christ. Emphasis throughout is on Christ's love of children. The quotations must have their setting in relation to the more detailed discussion of the Sacrament of the Holy Eucharist which is the main interest in this grade. The quotations follow:

"Thomas answered, and said to Him: My Lord, and my God" (John xx. 28).

"This is the Bread which cometh down from heaven; that if any man eat of it, he may not die" (John vi. 50).

"I am the living Bread which came down from heaven" (John vi. 51).

"In My Father's house there are many mansions. If not, I would have told you: because I go to prepare a place for you" (John xiv. 2).

"And if I shall go, and prepare a place for you, I will come again, and will take you to Myself: that where I am, you also may be" (John xiv. 3).

"Then they laid their hands upon them, and they received the Holy Ghost" (Acts viii. 17).

"Then were little children presented to Him, that He should impose hands upon them and pray. And the disciples rebuked them.

"But Jesus said to them: 'Suffer the little children, and forbid them not to come to Me: for the kingdom of heaven is for such'" (Matt. xix. 13, 14).

"If thou wilt enter into life, keep the Commandments" (Matt. xix. 17).

(The Ten Commandments.)

"If you will not forgive men, neither will your Father forgive you" (Matt. vi. 15).

"And taking bread, He gave thanks, and brake; and gave to them, saying: 'This is My body, which is given for you. Do this for a commemoration of Me.'

"In like manner the chalice also, after He had supped, saying: 'This is the chalice, the new testament in My blood, which shall be shed for you'" (Luke xxii. 19, 20).

"If any man eat of this Bread, he shall live for ever; and the Bread that I will give, is My flesh, for the life of the world" (John vi. 52).

"And Jesus said to them: I am the Bread of life: he that cometh to Me shall not hunger: and he that believeth in Me shall never thirst" (John vi. 35).

"And he that shall receive one such little child in My name, receiveth Me" (Matt. xviii. 5).

"My little children, let us not love in word, nor in tongue, but in deed and in truth" (I John iii. 18).

"As the Father hath loved Me, I also have loved you. Abide in My love" (John xv. 9).

"All the law is fulfilled in one word: Thou shalt love thy neighbor as thyself" (Gal. v. 14).

"Jesus answered, and said to him: If any one love Me, he will keep My word, and My Father will love him, and We will come to him, and will make Our abode with him" (John xiv. 23).

"Master, which is the great commandment in the law? Jesus said to him: 'Thou shalt love the Lord thy God with thy whole heart, and with thy whole soul, and with thy whole mind.' This is the greatest and the first commandment. And the second is like to this: 'Thou shalt love thy neighbor, as thyself.' On these two commandments dependeth the whole law and the prophets" (Matt. xxii. 36-40).

"This day thou shalt be with Me in Paradise" (Luke xxiii. 43).

Pictures

The children should know the following pictures, which should be presented in connection with the stories studied. Some should be made a matter of special study:

Christ Blessing Little Children — Plockhurst
Christ Blessing Little Children — Hoffmann
Suffer Little Children to Come Unto Me — Von Uhde
Christ Blessing Little Children — Vogel
Holy Family — Defregger
Christ and the Sinner — Hoffmann
Fourth Commandment — Senkel
Christ and the Rich Young Man — Hoffmann
Prodigal Son — Molitor

Good Shepherd — Plockhurst
Divine Shepherd — Murillo
Mary Magdalene — Hoffmann
The Crucifixion — Guido Reni
The Crucifixion — Hoffmann
The Crucifixion — Munkacsy
The Miracle of the Loaves and Fishes — Murillo
The Last Supper — Da Vinci
NOTE: *The Wonder Gifts,* by Marion Ames Taggart, contains many good pictures.

Activities

The oral and written language work supplementary to the material of this grade will naturally suggest itself, as well as the paper cutting, particularly in connection with the booklets hereafter proposed. A dramatization of the Prodigal Son would be especially appropriate for this grade. The pupils in this grade will make a booklet suggested by the following: My First Communion; Jesus My Best Friend; My Prayer Book; The Commandments. All pupils might prepare the first booklet and choose one of the others or still others suggested by the teacher or the child.

The Liturgy

The child will, in this grade, get two main ideas regarding the Mass: a *general* conception of the canon of the Mass; and the relation of the Mass to the Sacrifice on Calvary. He will learn the essential words of the consecration.

Poems

The poems in this grade center for the most part about the theme of the Child's Love of God, particularly in the Blessed Sacrament. If the child has made his Communion then this material should be used to renew, reënforce and revivify his love of God in the Blessed Sacrament and in practice the regularity of reception of this Sacrament. The suggestive collection of poems for this grade are:

Nails, Leonard Feeney, S.J.

God, Father John B. Tabb

The Way of the Cross, Leonard Feeney, S.J.

Christmas Song, Lydia A. C. Ward

The Holy Baby, Father Faber

One Summer Day, Margaret E. Jordan

Raindrops, Ellen Walsh

Gates and Doors, Joyce Kilmer

A Child's Prayer, M. Betham Edwards

Morning Prayer, Monsignor Robert Hugh Benson

The Name of Mary, Adelaide A. Procter

The Christ Child, G. K. Chesterton

The Annunciation, Adelaide A. Procter

Come to Jesus, Father Faber

Spring, Mary Dixon Thayer

Autumn, Mary Dixon Thayer

First Communion Day, Faber

God's Home, E. F. Garesché, S.J.

Holy Communion, Speer Strahan

The Lamb, William Blake

Finding You, Mary Dixon Thayer

Thoughts, Mary Dixon Thayer

I Like to Think the Days Are Steps, Mary Dixon Thayer

In the Morning, Mary Dixon Thayer

Winter, Mary Dixon Thayer

The King's Highway, Rev. Hugh F. Blunt

All Things Beautiful, John Keble

A Child's Morning Prayer, Mary L. Duncan

Sleep Song, Denis A. McCarthy

Saying Grace, Robert L. Stevenson

A Child's Wish, Rev. A. J. Ryan

Oh! Heaven, I Think, Must be Alway, Father Faber

Because He Loves Us, Alice Cary

A Christmas Gift, John Francis Quinn, S.J.
A Brave Man's Hope, Katherine E. Conway
O Sacred Cross! O Holy Tree!, William Cardinal O'Connell
Holy Ghost, Come Down Upon Thy Children, Father Faber
The Blessed Trinity, Rev. F. W. Faber

Some poems are placed in the later grades to serve
as a convenient opportunity to recall similar poems in
the earlier grades. In a particular grade the character
of the class will determine the nature of the treatment
of the poem; some poems will be read by the teacher,
some will be read in class, and referred to occasionally,
and some will be studied with great care. For the guidance of teachers there is listed in the syllabus, the
poems in previous grades which are similar to the individual poems studied in this grade.

Prayers

The more formal prayers to be taught are here
listed as a basis for work in this grade. Additional
prayers may be taught. The list is as follows:

1. Morning Prayers
2. Evening Prayers
3. Grace before meals
4. Grace after meals
5. Act of Contrition
6. Act of Faith
7. Act of Hope
8. Act of Charity

The "Our Father," the "Hail Mary," and the
"Angelus" will be recalled to mind frequently. The
"Angelus" will be said at noon.

Aspiration and Brief Prayers

As opportunity offers, the following aspirations or
others will be taught. One might be selected and

written on the board each month, calling attention to it as opportunity permits. The students might prepare aspirations of their own.

1. Eternal rest give unto them, O Lord, and let perpetual light shine upon them.
2. Sweet Heart of Jesus, be my love.
3. Sacred Heart of Jesus, I place my trust in Thee.
4. Lamb of God Who takest away the sins of the world, have mercy on us.
5. My Lord and my God.
6. May the Body and Blood of our Lord Jesus Christ preserve my soul to everlasting life.
7. My Jesus, mercy! Save me by Your Precious Blood.
8. Let us give thanks to the Lord, our God.
9. May the Almighty and merciful Lord grant us pardon, absolution, and remission of our sins.
10. Jesus, in the Most Holy Sacrament, have mercy on us.

Hymns

Hymns are an important factor in reënforcing the general religious instruction and training, valuable for their own content, and, if properly taught, add an element of joy to religious instruction that is quite important. The child should, at the end of instruction, know the great hymns of the Church. For the second grade there is suggested the following to be sung within the voice range of the children:

1. The Child's Prayer
2. Hymn to St. Joseph

3. A Child's Gift
4. A Child's May Hymn
5. While Shepherds Watched
6. A Child's Morning Prayer
7. The Child to the Guardian Angel
8. Jesus Teach Me How to Pray
9. O Lord, I am Not Worthy
10. Dear Angel, Ever at my Side
11. Mother Mary at Thine Altar
12. Mother, at Your Feet is Kneeling
13. Dear Guardian of Mary

Religious Practice

A definite part of the program in every grade is to build up the practice of religion in every grade and have the development cumulative throughout the grades. Wherever teachers see opportunity to build up Catholic practice they should do so. Teachers must not confound the lessons that may be essential and the actual practice in the life of the child. The pupil should understand the importance of interior disposition.

In the assignment to grade the purpose is to provide a specific time to see that the practice is established and understood. In some cases the habit will have been established. The cumulative listing of these practices is to emphasize the fact that they are not taught or established once and you are through with them. The practice must continue to be stimulated until it is "securely rooted in the life of the individual."

There should be emphasized in this grade:
1. Morning Prayer

2. Evening Prayer
3. Regular attendance at Mass on Sundays
4. Attendance at Mass on all holydays of obligation
5. Angelus
6. Bowing at the name of Jesus
7. Tipping hat or bowing as one passes church
8. Tipping hat when one meets Priest or Sister or other religious
9. Monthly Communion or more frequently

Practical Life

The translation of the religious knowledge practice and attitudes in the day-to-day life of the child must always be an objective in religious education. The elevation of the actual daily life of the individual to a supernatural plane will come about through the character of the individual's motivation. This must be a matter of development; the child must be taken, however, where he is. The lines of development are indicated but the more specific content is left for the experimentation of the first year. A teacher should always take advantage of any actual situation, and should always strive to meet difficulties which her children as a group are confronted with, no matter whether it is included in the course or not.

1. Do a good turn every day for the love of God.
    a) Daily examination of conscience at night.
    b) Daily specific review of day's thoughts, words, or deeds.
    c) Weekly complete examination of conscience for confession or as a preparation for spiritual Communion.

    d) Daily expiation for the temporal punishment due to sin.

2. Cultivation of virtuous life.

3. Cultivation of school virtues.

4. Promotion of corporal and spiritual works of mercy.

Special attention is directed to the chapters on "The Christian Rule of Life" and "The Christian Daily Exercise" of the *Catechism of Christian Doctrine* approved by the Cardinal, Archbishops, and Bishops of England and Wales, and directed to be used in all their dioceses.[1]

Christian Doctrine

The formal teaching of doctrine is the main interest of the seventh and eighth grades, but that will not be the child's first contact with the doctrine. He meets it frequently at various levels, and from various angles throughout the course. He organizes this knowledge and experience in the seventh and eighth grades. We call attention here, for example, in a general way to the doctrinal content of this grade, even though the method of teaching is not the ordinary formal method.

In this grade the child receives the general groundwork of Christian doctrine: God the Father, the Creation, Adam and Eve, original sin, the commandments of God, actual sin, the Redemption, the Resurrection, the Church, the Sacrifice of the Mass, the Sacraments of Baptism, Penance (including Confession), and Confirmation.

---

[1]This is printed herewith, but is reserved for formal study in the seventh and eighth grades in the discretion of the Pastor.

As far as the creed is concerned they have the following: I believe (1) in God, the Father, (2) in Jesus Christ, His Son, (3) in the Holy Ghost, (4) in one God in three Divine Persons, (5) in the Holy Catholic Church, and (6) in the forgiveness of sins.

Basal Texts and Supplementary Material

An experimental text has been worked out for this grade called *The Life of the Soul* (Bruce). This text, besides certain fundamental information, will deal with baptism, penance, the Eucharist, and confirmation. It will include the material covered in Cardinal Gaspari's *Catechism for Children about to be Admitted to Holy Communion*. It conforms to the rule of the decree on Holy Communion of Pope Pius X. Father Kelley's *Our First Communion* (Benziger) is recommended as a supplementary text. Supplementary material will be found in:

Loyola, Mother, *First Communion*, Burns and Oates.
Loyola, Mother, *Jesus of Nazareth*, Benziger.
Sisters of Notre Dame, *First Communion Day*, Herder.
Eaton, Mary, *The Little Ones*, Herder.
Brownson, J. Van Dyke, *To the Heart of a Child*, Universal Knowledge Foundation.
Matimore, Rev. P. Henry, *A Child's Garden of Religious Stories*, pp. 243–260, Macmillan.
Sisters of Notre Dame, *Thoughts and Prayers for First Communion*, Herder.
Taggart, Marion Ames, *The Wonder Gifts*, Benziger.
Sisters of St. Dominic, *My Gift to Jesus*, Lawdale.
de Zulueta, Rev. F. M., *Child Prepared for First Communion*, Benziger.
Eleanore, Sister M., *The Little Flower's Love for the Holy Eucharist*, Benziger.

The Christian's Rule of Life

I

What Rule of Life Must We Follow if We Hope to be Saved?

If we hope to be saved, we must follow the rule of life taught by Jesus Christ.

What Are We Bound to Do by the Rule of Life Taught by Jesus Christ?

By the rule of life taught by Jesus Christ we are bound always to hate sin and to love God.

How Must We Hate Sin?

We must hate sin above all other evils, so as to be resolved never to commit a willful sin, for the love or fear of anything whatsoever.

How Must We Love God?

We must love God above all things, and with our whole heart.

How Must We Learn to Love God?

We must learn to love God by begging of God to teach us to love Him: "O my God, teach me to love Thee."

II

What Will the Love of God Lead Us to Do?

The love of God will lead us often to think how good God is; often to speak to Him in our hearts and always to seek to please Him.

Does Jesus Christ Also Command Us to Love One Another?

Jesus Christ also commands us to love one another — that is, all persons, without exception — for His sake.

How Are We to Love One Another?

We are to love one another by wishing well to one another, and praying for one another; and by never allowing ourselves any thought, word, or deed to the injury of anyone.

Are We Also Bound to Love Our Enemies?

We are also bound to love our enemies, not only by forgiving them from our hearts, but also by wishing them well, and praying for them.

Has Jesus Christ Given Us Another Great Rule?

Jesus Christ has given us another great rule in these words: "If any man will come after Me, let him deny himself, and take up his cross daily, and follow Me" (Luke ix. 23).

How Are We to Deny Ourselves?

We are to deny ourselves by giving up our own will, and by going against our own humors, inclinations, and passions.

Why Are We Bound to Deny Ourselves?

We are bound to deny ourselves because our natural inclinations are prone to evil from our very childhood; and, if not corrected by self-denial, they will certainly carry us to hell.

How Are We to Take Up Our Cross Daily?

We are to take up our cross daily by submitting daily with patience to the labors and sufferings of this short life, and by bearing them willingly for the love of God.

III

How Are We to Follow Our Blessed Lord?

We are to follow our Blessed Lord by walking in His footsteps and imitating His virtues.

What Are the Principal Virtues We Are to Learn of Our Blessed Lord?

The principal virtues we are to learn of our Blessed Lord are: meekness, humility, and obedience.

Which Are the Enemies We Must Fight Against All the Days of Our Life?

The enemies which we must fight against all the days of our life are: the devil, the world, and the flesh.

What Do You Mean by the Devil?

By the devil I mean Satan and all his wicked angels, who are ever seeking to draw us into sin, that we may be damned with them.

What Do You Mean by the World?

By the world I mean the false maxims of the world, and the society of those who love the vanities, riches, and pleasures of this world better than God.

Why Do You Number the Devil and the World Among the Enemies of the Soul?

I number the devil and the world among the enemies of the soul because they are always seeking by temptation, and by word or example, to carry us along with them in the broad road that leads to damnation.

What Do You Mean by the Flesh?

By the flesh, I mean our own corrupt inclinations and passions, which are the most dangerous of all our enemies.

What Must We Do to Hinder the Enemies of Our Soul from Drawing Us Into Sin?

To hinder the enemies of our soul from drawing us into sin, we must watch, pray, and fight against all their suggestions and temptations.

In the Warfare Against the Devil, the World, and the Flesh on Whom Must We Depend?

In the warfare against the devil, the world, and the flesh we must depend, not on ourselves, but on God only: "I can do all things in Him Who strengtheneth me" (Phil. iv. 13).

IV

The Christian's Daily Exercise

How Should You Begin the Day?

I should begin the day by making the Sign of the Cross as soon as I awake in the morning, and by saying some short prayer, such as: "O my God, I offer my heart and soul to Thee."

How Should You Rise in the Morning?

I should rise in the morning diligently, dress myself modestly, and then kneel down and say my morning prayers.

Should You Also Hear Mass if You Have Time and Opportunity?

I should also hear Mass if I have time and opportunity, for to hear Mass is by far the best and most profitable of all devotions.

Is It Useful to Make Daily Meditation?

It is useful to make daily meditation, for such was the practice of all the saints.

On What Ought We to Meditate?

We ought to meditate especially on the four last things, and the life and passion of our Blessed Lord.

Ought We Frequently to Read Good Books?

We ought frequently to read good books, such as the Holy Gospels, the Lives of the Saints, and other spiritual works, which nourish our faith and piety, and arm us against the false maxims of the world.

And What Should You Do as to Your Eating, Drinking, Sleeping, and Amusements?

As to my eating, drinking, sleeping, and amusements, I should use all these things with moderation, and with a desire to please God.

Say the Grace Before Meals.

"Bless us, O Lord, and these Thy gifts, which we are going to receive from Thy bounty, through Christ our Lord. Amen."

Say Grace After Meals.

"We give Thee thanks, Almighty God, for all Thy benefits, Who livest and reignest, world without end. Amen. May the souls of the faithful departed, through the mercy of God, rest in peace. Amen."

How Should You Sanctify Your Ordinary Actions and Employments of the Day?

I should sanctify my ordinary actions and employments of the day by often raising up my heart to God whilst I am about them, and saying some short prayer to Him.

What Should You do When You Find Yourself Tempted to Sin?

When I find myself tempted to sin I should make the Sign of the Cross on my heart, and call on God as earnestly as I can, saying "Lord, save me, or I perish."

If You Have Fallen Into Sin, What Should You Do?

If I have fallen into sin, I should cast myself in spirit at the feet of Christ, and humbly beg His pardon by a sincere act of contrition.

When God Sends You Any Cross, or Sickness, or Pain, What Should You Say?

When God sends me any cross, or sickness, or pain, I should say, "Lord, Thy will be done; I take this for my sins."

What Little Indulgenced Prayers Would You do Well to Say Often to Yourself During the Day?

I should do well to say often to myself during the day such little indulgenced prayers as:

"Glory be to the Father, and to the Son, and to the Holy Ghost; as it was in the beginning, is now, and ever shall be, world without end. Amen."

"In all things may the most holy, the most just, and the most lovable will of God be done, praised, and exalted above all for ever."

"O Sacrament most holy, O Sacrament, Divine, all praise and all thanksgiving be every moment Thine."

"Praised be Jesus Christ, praised for evermore."

"My Jesus, mercy; Mary, help."

How Should You Finish the Day?

I should finish the day by kneeling down and saying my night prayers.

After Your Night Prayers What Should You Do?

After my night prayers I should observe due modesty in going to bed; occupy myself with the thoughts of death; and endeavor to compose myself to rest at the foot of the cross, and give my last thoughts to my crucified Savior.

RELIGION IN GRADE IV

Main Interest: Old Testament History

THE content of the fourth grade centers around Bible history. In order to bring it within the experience of the child, it will be told in a series of biographies. In order to provide for connection and continuity, either the text or the teacher will provide the account of the situation in which the principal figure was concerned. In this way an adequate historical background will be furnished for each character and historical continuity provided.

The characters and topics selected for study are:

Outline of Main Topics

I. *Creation of the World*
   1. The creation
   2. Adam and Eve
   3. Cain and Abel
   4. Noah

II. *The Founders*
   1. Abraham
   2. Melchisedech
   3. Isaac
   4. Jacob
   5. Joseph
   6. Job

III. *The Time of Moses*
IV. *The Time of Josue and Judges*
  1. Gideon
  2. Ruth
  3. Samuel
 V. *The Great Kings*
  1. Saul
  2. David
  3. Solomon
VI. *The Time of the Great Prophets*
  1. Elias
  2. Eliseus
  3. Tobias
  4. Isaiah
  5. Jeremias
VII. *The Babylonian Captivity*
  1. Ezechiel
  2. Daniel
VIII. *After the Babylonian Captivity*
  1. Esther
  2. Judith
  3. Judas the Machabee

The purpose of this study is not a complete history of the Jews, but a review of the principal characters in Jewish religious history, with emphasis on biography. The main points to be secured are three: (1) the conception of a Messiah in Jewish history, with the Messianic prophecies; (2) the situation among the Jews at the time of Christ, and (3) the basis for their rejection of Christ. It will be a real challenge to the ingenuity and skill of both textbook and teacher to do this.

Quotations

In this grade the quotations to be memorized relate especially to the Messianic prophecies; some others of significance as a preparation for the Mass. Some quotations are given to illustrate the wisdom literature of the Jews. A few psalms are added for their significance in themselves as well as to illustrate the work of David the singer; others may be substituted:

"But Melchisedech the king of Salem, bringing forth bread and wine, for he was the priest of the most high God. Blessed him, and said: Blessed be Abram by the most high God, Who created heaven and earth" (Gen. xiv, 18–19).

"Who is there among you, that will shut the doors, and will kindle the fire on My altar gratis? I have no pleasure in you, saith the Lord of hosts: and I will not receive a gift of your hand. For from the rising of the sun even to the going down, My Name is great among the Gentiles, and in every place there is sacrifice, and there is offered to My Name a clean oblation: for My Name is great among the Gentiles, saith the Lord of hosts" (Mal. i, 10–11).

Psalm lxxxix.

Psalm lii.

"The voice of one crying in the desert: Prepare ye the way of the Lord, make straight in the wilderness the paths of our God" (Isa. xl, 3).

"For a CHILD IS BORN to us, and a Son is given to us, and the government is upon His shoulder: and His Name shall be called, Wonderful, Counsellor, God the Mighty, the Father of the world to come, the Prince of Peace" (Isa. ix, 6).

"Therefore the Lord Himself shall give you a sign. Behold a virgin shall conceive, and bear a Son, and His Name shall be called Emmanuel" (Isa. vii, 14).

"Behold My Servant, I will uphold Him: My elect, My soul delighteth in Him: I have given My spirit upon Him. He shall bring forth judgment to the Gentiles" (Isa. xlii, 1).

"They parted My garments amongst them; and upon My vesture they cast lots" (Ps. xxi, 19).

"And I said to them: If it be good in your eyes, bring hither my wages: and if not, be quiet. And they weighed for my wages thirty pieces of silver" (Zach. xi, 12).

"They shall not leave anything thereof until morning, nor break a bone thereof, they shall observe all the ceremonies of the phase" (Num. ix, 12).

"AND THOU, BETHLEHEM Ephrata, art a little one among the thousands of Juda: out of thee shall He come forth unto Me that is to be the ruler in Israel: and His going forth *is* from the beginning, from the days of eternity" (Mic. v, 2).

"Judge me, O God, and distinguish my cause from the nation that is not holy: deliver me from the unjust and deceitful man.

For Thou art God my strength: why hast Thou cast me off? and why do I go sorrowful whilst the enemy afflicteth me?

Send forth Thy light and Thy truth: they have conducted me, and have brought me unto Thy holy hill, and into Thy tabernacles.

And I will go into the altar of God: to God Who giveth joy to my youth.

To Thee, O God my God, I will give praise upon the harp: why art thou sad, O my soul? and why dost thou disquiet me?

Hope in God, for I will still give praise to Him: the salvation of my countenance, and my God" (Ps. xlii, 1–6).

"I will wash my hands among the innocent; and will compass Thy altar, O Lord:

That I may hear the voice of Thy praise: and tell of all Thy wondrous works.

I have loved, O Lord, the beauty of Thy house; and the place where Thy glory dwelleth.

Take not away my soul, O God, with the wicked: nor my life with bloody men:

In whose hands are iniquities: their right hand is filled with gifts" (Ps. xxv, 6–10).

"And one of the Seraphims flew to me, and in his hand was a live coal, which he had taken with the tongs off the altar.

And he touched my mouth, and said: Behold this hath touched thy lips, and thy iniquities shall be taken away, and thy sin shall be cleansed" (Isa. vi, 6–7).

"Blessed art Thou, O Lord the God of our fathers: and worthy to be praised, and glorified, and exalted above all for ever: and blessed is the holy name of Thy glory: and worthy to be praised, and exalted above all in all ages" (Dan. iii, 52).

"The fear of the Lord is the beginning of wisdom. Fools despise wisdom and instruction" (Prov. i, 7).

"My son, hear the instruction of thy father, and forsake not the law of thy mother" (Prov. i, 8).

"My son, forget not My law, and let thy heart keep My commandments" (Prov. iii, 1).

"For whom the Lord loveth, He chastiseth: and as a father in the son He pleaseth Himself" (Prov. iii, 12).

"Go to the ant, O sluggard, and consider her ways, and learn wisdom" (Prov. vi, 6).

"Six things there are, which the Lord hateth, and the seventh His soul detesteth:

Haughty eyes, a lying tongue, hands that shed innocent blood.

A heart that deviseth wicked plots, feet that are swift to run into mischief.

A deceitful witness that uttereth lies, and him that soweth discord among brethren" (Prov. vi, 16–19).

"My son, keep my words, and lay up my precepts with thee. Son, keep the commandments, and thou shalt live: and my law as the apple of thy eye:

Bind it upon thy fingers, write it upon the tables of thy heart" (Prov. vii, 1–3).

Activities

The stories of the Old Testament offer excellent opportunities for spontaneous dramatization in the classroom, and for a more formal literary dramatization. Suggestions are contained in Sr. Aurelia and Fr. Kirsch's *Practical Aids for Catholic Teachers,* pp. 234–238. Suggestive dramatizations are offered (pp. 238–242) of

Cain and Abel

The Building of the Ark

Noah's Offering — the Rainbow

The Story of Joseph

The Story of Moses*

The student might select a special character in Old Testament history to make a booklet about him or her, presenting orally to the class toward the end of the semester or year a summary of what he learned. Sand-table projects, posters, calendars, booklets, plays, stories, collection of poems, pictures, even movies furnish fresh methods of approach, or methods of reënforcing more conventional methods of learning.

Pictures

For the picture study of this grade, reënforcing the main topic of the grade, there are two excellent sources of material. First are the 120 Old Testament pictures by J. James Tissot, published by the American Tissot Society, and another are the pictures by Gustave Doré illustrating the Paradise lost. For textbook pictures we have already referred you to the pictures in the *Katholische Schulbibel* by Fügel. In this grade students should become acquainted with Sargeant's *Prophets.*

---

*The steps in analyzing a story either in preparation for a dramatization or for writing a biography are illustrated in the article, by Miss Margaret Canty, "Joseph the Dreamer" in the March, 1931, issue of the CATHOLIC SCHOOL JOURNAL.

Religious Vocabulary

Special care must be taken to see that the child's religious vocabulary is increased in connection particularly with the main topic of the grade, and that the new words are taught as the need develops and in the actual situation. Care should be taken to review words previously learned and to be sure a correct meaning is given to them on the child's own level. The words should grow in connotation as his religious knowledge and experience increase.

Words that will generally be taught in this grade are:

Messiah (Messias)	psalm	prophet
prophecy	Genesis	disobedience
sacrifice	Babel	famine
Pharaoh	plagues	Sinai
tables of stone	idolatry	manna
ingratitude	bondage	deliverance
priest	anointed	sanctuary
Ark of the Covenant	captivity	Babylon (ion)
miracles	sacred scriptures	Pharisees
Paradise	Palestine	Israel
Juda		

Each teacher will be required to make up her specific lists for her specific children. No stress need be placed on the spelling of these words. They may be left on the board for reference.

Poems

The poems suggested for the fourth grade carrying along the fundamental idea of the curriculum and

furnishing reënforcement for the central interest of
this grade are:

Father in Heaven, We Thank Thee
The Word True, Sister Agnes Finley
This Above All to Thine Own Self be True, Shakespeare
Our Heavenly Father, Rev. Frederick W. Faber
Absolom, Nathaniel Parker Willis
Psalm 150, David
The Meadow of Prayer, Edward F. Garesché, S.J.
That Holy Thing, George MacDonald
Worship Old and New, S. M. Pierre
By the Waters of Babylon, Christina Rossetti
Heroes, Denis A. McCarthy
St. Peter, Eileen Duggan
A Sorrowful Sigh of a Prisoner, C. Rossetti
Mary Magdalene, Christina Rossetti
The Catechism of the Clock, Eleanor C. Donnelly
Why the Robin's Breast was Red, James Ryder Randall
Wishes for My Son, Thomas MacDonagh
The Helper, Rev. Hugh Francis Blunt
My Wish, Rev. Francis J. Butler
Each Daily Task, Very Rev. T. L. Crowley, O.P.
A Christmas Carol, Adelaide A. Procter
All of It, Rev. Hugh Francis Blunt
The Mother's Quest, Rev. Hugh Francis Blunt
The Burial of Moses, Cecil Frances Alexander
Adam and Eve, Progressive Series, Third Reader
Evening Prayer, William Allingham
As Little Children, William V. Doyle, S.J.
Mistletoe, Rev. John B. Tabb
A Child's Thought of God, Elizabeth Barrett Browning
The Children and the Angels, Mary E. Mannix
Content and Rich, Rev. Robert Southwell, S.J.
The Vision of Baltassar, Lord Byron
Guardian Angel, Cardinal Newman
Christmas, Nahum Tate
Ballad of Trees and the Master, Sidney Lanier
Blessed Candle, Joseph Kinney Collins

He was the Word that Spake It, John Donne
The Caliph's Magnanimity
A Legend
A Child's Evening Prayer, Samuel Taylor Coleridge
How Children Should Live, Isaac Watts
The Queen of May
Sheep and Lambs, Katharine Tynan
Speak Little Voice, Rev. Michael Earls, S.J.
Holy Communion, Speer Strahan

Additional poems should be used emphasizing the public life of Christ which is the center of interest in the grade. Children should be encouraged to "learn by heart" as many poems as possible. All should be required to learn some; many of the poems should be left to the student's own taste. The more difficult poems will be read to the class by the teachers; some poems will be read for their general idea without detailed study, and some poems will be studied in detail. Poems dealing with the same subject in earlier grades should be recalled to mind after the first reading of new poems. The poems suggested above, with others, are included in *Religious Poems for Children, Intermediate Grades,* (Bruce).

Aspirations and Brief Prayers

As opportunity offers, the following aspirations and brief prayers or others will be taught. One might be selected and written on the board each month, calling attention to it as opportunity permits. The Psalms furnish an almost inexhaustible source for additional suggestions. The students might prepare aspirations of their own. The following are selected from the Old Testament:

1. Have mercy on me and hear my prayer (Ps. iv).

2. O Lord, my God, in Thee have I put my trust: save me from all them that persecute me and deliver me (Ps. vii).

3. I will give praise to Thee, O Lord, with my whole heart (Ps. ix).

4. Preserve me, O Lord, for I have put my trust in Thee (Ps. xv).

5. My God *is* my helper, and in Him will I put my trust (Ps. xvii).

6. To Thee, O Lord, have I lifted up my soul. In Thee, O my God, I put my trust, let me not be ashamed (Ps. xxiv).

7. I will bless the Lord at all times. His praise shall be always in my mouth (Ps. xxxiii).

8. Forsake me not, O Lord my God: do not Thou depart from me. Attend unto my help, O Lord, the God of my salvation (Ps. xxxvii).

9. Have mercy on me, O God, according to Thy great mercy (Ps. l).

10. Blessed art Thou, O Lord the God of our fathers; and worthy to be praised, and glorified, and exalted above all for ever: and blessed is the holy name of Thy glory: and worthy to be praised, and exalted above all in all ages (Dan. iii. 52).

11. And now, O Lord, think of me, and take not revenge of my sins, neither remember my offences nor those of my parents (Tob. iii. 3).

Prayers

As the child develops, the form of prayers he will learn will change. The form of morning prayer will undoubtedly change from the simplest form to the use of the liturgical prayers of the Church. This will be generally the development. There will be, of course, an increase in the number of prayers, so that by the end of the elementary school the student will be acquainted with the principal prayers of the Church.

1. Morning Prayers
2. Evening Prayers
3. Grace before meals
4. Grace after meals
5. Act of Contrition
6. Act of Faith
7. Act of Hope
8. Act of Charity
9. Stations of the Cross
10. The Gloria
11. Prayers of thanksgiving and praise from the Psalms

Hymns

Hymns are an important factor in reënforcing the general religious instruction and training, valuable for their own content, and, if properly taught, add an element of joy in religious instruction that is quite important. The child should, at the end of instruction, know the great hymns of the Church. For the fourth grade there is suggested the following to be sung within the voice range of the children:

1. Canticle of the Three Children (Dan. iii. 26)
2. Benedicite (Dan. iii. 57)
3. O Come, O Come, Emmanuel
4. Drop Down, Dew

5. God the Father, Who Didst Make Me
6. Souls of Men Why Will Ye Scatter
7. How Blind Thou Art
8. Jerusalem The Golden
9. Now Doth the Sun Ascend the Sky
10. Sing Praise to God
11. God, the Only Good

Liturgy

The main interest of this grade will be the history of the Jews in the Old Testament, and will furnish valuable concrete information regarding the sacrifice in the religious sense. It would therefore seem to be desirable to emphasize in this grade the Christian altar and its ornaments, and incidentally other parts of the Church, the credence table, the Communion rail, the pulpit, the baptistery, and the sacristy.

Useful supplementary material for the study of various aspects of the liturgy will be found in Father Dunney's *The Mass*, (Macmillan Co.), and Father M. S. MacMahon's *Liturgical Catechism*, (Gill & Son, Dublin), and *St. Andrew's Missal*.

Religious Information

There are certain facts about religious persons, vestments, ceremonies, and institutions that are a part of the equipment of every cultivated person, as well as essential or at least supplementary to religious practice. These need to be taught, and specific provision should be made for the instruction.

One is surprised often to find adults who do not know what INRI means, or *Alpha* and *Omega*, or even IHS, why the Mass is said in Latin, or who some prominent character in the Old or New Testament is. The teacher should use every opportunity to give such information whenever she discovers there is need for it.

In this grade will be taught, in addition to what the teacher discovers to be the need of the pupil, the following:

Facts about the Old Testament

  I. The Books of the Old Testament
    1. The Historical Books (Genesis to Esther)
    2. Poetical Books (Job to Ecclesiasticus)
      a) Poetical
      b) Didactic
    3. The Prophetical Books (Isaias to Malachias)
      a) Major
      b) Minor
    4. Supplementary, Historical (1–2 Machabees)
  II. Divine Inspiration of the Bible
 III. Books in the Catholic Bible omitted in Protestant Version
 IV. Priesthood and Sacrifice in Old Testament
  V. Hebrew measures and money
    1. Shekels, drachmas, bin, etc.

An indispensable guide to the teacher is Pope's *The Catholic Student's Aids to the Studies of the Bible*, Vol. I (Rev. Ed.), which includes an English translation of Pope Leo XIII's Encyclical on the Study of the Bible, *Providentissimus Deus*, and also Vol. II.

A specially useful source of questions and answers for this part of the course on religious information is Father John F. Sullivan's *Externals of the Catholic*

Church, Her Government, Ceremonies, Festivals, Sacramentals and Devotions (Kenedy), and Father Conway's *The Question Box.* The new *Catholic Dictionary* is especially useful. For reference the *Catholic Encyclopedia* is indispensable.

This heading is placed in the curriculum so that the teacher will realize the relative importance of this informational background to the main purpose, and will not give it undue emphasis at the expense of weightier matters. Information should be given as information.

Religious Practice

A definite part of the program in every grade is to build up the practice of religion in every grade and have the development cumulative throughout the grades. Wherever teachers see opportunity to build up Catholic practice, they should do so. Teachers must not confound the lessons that may be essential and the actual practice in the life of the child. The pupil should understand the importance of interior disposition.

In the assignment to grade the purpose is to provide a specific time to see that the practice is established and understood. In some cases the habit will have been established. The cumulative listing of these practices is to emphasize the fact that they are not taught or established once and you are through with them. The practice must continue to be stimulated until it is "securely rooted in the life of the individual." There should be emphasized in this grade:

1. Morning Prayer
2. Evening Prayer

3. Regular attendance at Mass on Sundays
4. Attendance at Mass on all holydays of obligation
5. Angelus
6. Bowing at the name of Jesus
7. Tipping hat or bowing as one passes church
8. Tipping hat when one meets Priest or Sister or other religious
9. Monthly Communion or more frequently
10. Keeping spirit of Lent by sacrifice
11. Saying Stations of the Cross

Practical Life

The translation of the religious knowledge, practice, and attitudes in the day-to-day life of the child must always be an objective in religious education. The elevation of the actual daily life of the individual to a supernatural plane will come about through the character of the individual's motivation. This must be a matter of development; the child must be taken, however, where he is. The lines of development are indicated but the more specific content is left for the experimentation of the first year. A teacher should always take advantage of any actual situation, and should always strive to meet difficulties which her children as a group are confronted with, no matter whether it is included in the course of study or not.

1. Do a good turn every day for the love of God.
   a) Daily examination of conscience at night.
   b) Daily specific review of day's thoughts, words, or deeds.
   c) Weekly complete examination of conscience

for confession or as a preparation for spiritual Communion.

   d) Daily expiation for the temporal punishment due to sin.
2. Cultivation of virtuous life.
3. Cultivation of school virtues.
4. Promotion of corporal and spiritual works of mercy.

Special attention is directed to the chapters on "The Christian Rule of Life" and "The Christian Daily Exercise" of the *Catechism of Christian Doctrine* approved by the Cardinal, Archbishops, and Bishops of England and Wales, and directed to be used in all their dioceses.

Christian Doctrine

In this grade Christ is studied as He is anticipated in the Old Testament. God's relation with the Hebrew people generally is the content. The Ten Commandments are reviewed here in their historical setting. The visits of angels to earth are met concretely here as a basis for later study of angels, and in review of first-grade material. The Messianic prophecies and in general the expectation of Israel are emphasized. The prayers of the Old Testament are noted in the Psalms particularly, and particularly in such portions of them as are found in the Mass.

Texts and Teaching Material

An adequate basal text on the Old Testament in the fourth-grade level is not now available. The syllabus contains the detailed outline of the instruction.

It is expected that the experience of the first year will give an adequate basis for a text especially prepared for the course written with a biographical emphasis.

The following newer texts may prove useful:

Bible Stories for Children, Sister Anna Louise.

Bible History of the Old and New Testament with Compendium of Church History, Sister Anna Louise.

Compendium of Bible and Church History, Brother Eugene.

Illustrated Bible History, Rev. Ignatius Schuster.

A Child's Garden of Religion Stories, Rev. P. Henry Matimore.

Wonder Stories of God's People, Rev. P. Henry Matimore.

Old Testament Rhymes, Rev. Robert Hugh Benson, (Longmans Green & Co.).

The Bible Story, Rev. George Johnson, Rev. Jerome D. Hannan, and Sr. M. Dominica, O.S.U. (to be followed by *Bible History* and *Church History*).

Valuable suggestions may be secured from stories in school readers. A partial list indicating range and technique of material is given at the end of this grade.

RELIGION IN GRADE V

Main Interest: Church History

THE center of interest in the fifth grade is the history of the Church told in a series of biographies of popular saints, and other Catholic leaders. It is especially important here that nothing shall be taught which needs to be unlearned. The teacher might read with profit for a general point of view Belloc's *The Catholic Church and History*.

Point of View

It is possible at this level to give a child a historical sense of the greatness of the Church's followers. It is this sense of the greatness, the stability, and the security of the Church that the students will get through the biographies. The teacher must feel this, else it cannot be communicated very well. A paragraph in Father Guilday's *An Introduction to Church History* is copied here for the teacher's guidance:

"Out of it all — out of the tremendous past of the Church, out of the certainties and uncertainties that crowd its pages, one fact looms high in historical value: if ever there was a power or an institution on earth which should long since have perished from the memory of man, that power and that institution is the Catholic Church. What has not been done to destroy it? A hundred times in the past twenty centuries has the Church of God stood on the verge of utter collapse. So has it seemed to human eyes. But the standard set up in the midst of the nations remains forever erect, strengthening its adherents with the unfaltering assurance that their Faith is founded upon a rock, solid and impregnable. In its infancy in the Jewish synagogues of a dying Israel, amid the unspeakable perils of the Roman persecutions, in the depths of the catacombs, under the dead weight of the barbarian blight, in the subtle toils of feudal encroachments, in the presence of the mighty tyranny of a new Cæsarism, in the dark night of the cleavage during the sixteenth century, amid the enmities of Protestant nations and the uncertain friendships of Catholic nations, down to these days of our own, the struggle for liberty of action and independence for spiritual conquest has never ceased. But through it all and in it all and in spite of all that has been attempted to thwart the onward march of her progress, the Church has been victorious. This, then, is the foremost lesson of her history: the unconquerable stability of the Catholic Faith."

There is a quotation in Father Guilday's book from Père Delehaye's *Legends of the Saints* that might very well guide the teacher in the selection of her material for the biographies. It is:

"Historical criticism, when applied to the lives of the saints, has had certain results which are in no way surprising to those who are accustomed to handle documents and to interpret inscriptions, but which have had a somewhat disturbing effect on the mind of the general public. . . . If you suggest that the biographer of a saint has been unequal to his task, or that he has not professed to write as a historian, you are accused of attacking the saint himself, who, it appears, is too powerful to allow himself to be compromised by an indiscreet panegyrist. If, again, you venture to express doubt concerning certain marvelous incidents repeated by the author on insufficient evidence, although well calculated to enhance the glory of the saint, you are at once suspected of lack of faith. You are told you are introducing the spirit of rationalism into history, as though in questions of fact it were not above all things essential to weigh the evidence. How often has not an accusation of destructive criticism been flung, and men treated as iconoclasts, whose sole object has been to appraise at their true value the documents which justify our attitude of veneration, and who are only too happy when able to declare that one of God's friends has been fortunate enough to find a historian worthy of his task."

Outline of Main Topics

The content of the fifth grade will center around the history of the Church. Starting out with the life of Christ as the foundation of the life of the Church, and supplementing it with the lives and statements of Paul and Peter, the pupil will then study the great personalities in the development of the Church in biographical form. Each personality is selected especially for the points listed in the detailed syllabus which supplements this course of study. Here as in the fourth grade the teacher will provide if the text does not, the historical situation in which the character acted, and in this way emphasize historical backgrounds and secure historical continuity.

A. *Founding of Church*
   1. Christ, the Foundation
   2. St. Peter, the Rock
B. *Early Development*
   1. St. Paul
   2. Timothy
   3. St. Stephen and Other Early Martyrs
   4. St. Augustine and the Church Fathers
   5. Council of Nicea
   6. Conversion of Constantine
C. *Development of Monasticism*
   1. St. Anthony
   2. St. Benedict
D. *The Crusades*
   1. Mohammed and Mohammedans
   2. Pope Urban and the Crusades
   3. Lay Leaders
E. *Development of Papacy*
   1. Gregory
   2. Innocent
F. *Great Saints of Middle Ages*
   1. St. Thomas Aquinas
   2. St. Dominic
   3. St. Francis of Assisi
   4. St. Bernard
G. *The Revolution*
   1. St. Ignatius Loyola
   2. The Council of Trent
H. *Founding of Schools*
   1. The Popes and the Universities
   2. Blessed de la Salle
   3. The Church and Art

a) Dante
b) Michelangelo
c) The Cathedral Builders

I. *The Extension of the Church Missions*
1. St. Paul
2. St. Patrick
3. St. Boniface
4. St. Francis Xavier
5. Modern Missionaries

J. *Definition of Two Doctrines*
1. The Infallibility of the Pope
2. The Immaculate Conception

K. *Church Relation to Social Question*
1. Leo XIII
2. St. Vincent de Paul

L. *Recent Saints*
1. St. Thérèse, the Little Flower
2. The Jesuit Martyrs of North America

M. *Great Catholic Laymen*
1. Ozanam

N. *The Church and Peace*
1. Benedict XV and the World War

Quotations

The quotations in this grade center on the nature and characteristics of the Church. Here as in preceding grades the quotations will not be taught as unrelated quotations assigned for memorizing, but significant statements conveniently summarizing some fact or the significant basis of doctrines. In this grade particularly, the teacher should be satisfied if the child gets the fundamental idea. Theological discussion is not desirable or necessary. Subsequent study in this curriculum provides for recalling to mind these passages within the elementary-school period. The significant quotations are:

"For if the blood of goats and of oxen, and the ashes of an heifer being sprinkled, sanctify such as are defiled, to the cleansing of the flesh:

"How much more shall the blood of Christ, Who by the Holy Ghost offered Himself unspotted unto God, cleanse our conscience from dead works, to serve the living God?" (Heb. ix. 12–14.)

"Amen, amen, I say unto you: He that believeth in Me, hath everlasting life.

I am the bread of life.

Your fathers did eat manna in the desert, and are dead.

This is the bread which cometh down from heaven that if any man eat of it, he may not die.

I am the living bread which came down from heaven.

If any man eat of this bread, he shall live for ever; and the bread that I will give, is My flesh, for the life of the world.

The Jews, therefore, strove among themselves, saying: How can this man give us His flesh to eat?

Then Jesus said to them: Amen, amen, I say unto you: Except you eat the flesh of the Son of man, and drink His blood, you shall not have life in you.

He that eateth My flesh, and drinketh My blood, hath everlasting life: and I will raise him up in the last day.

For My flesh is meat indeed: and My blood is drink indeed.

He that eateth My flesh, and drinketh My blood, abideth in Me, and I in him.

As the living Father hath sent Me, and I live by the Father; so he that eateth Me, the same also shall live by Me.

This is the bread that came down from heaven. Not as your fathers did eat manna, and are dead. He that eateth this bread, shall live for ever.

These things He said, teaching in the synagogue, in Capharnaum" (John vi. 47–60).

"And Jesus coming, spoke to them, saying: All power is given to Me in heaven and in earth.

Going therefore, teach ye all nations; baptizing them in the name of the Father, and of the Son, and of the Holy Ghost.

Teaching them to observe all things whatsoever I have commanded you: and behold I am with you all days, even to the consummation of the world" (Matt. xxviii. 18–20).

"But you shall receive the power of the Holy Ghost coming upon you, and you shall be witnesses unto Me in Jerusalem, and in all Judea, and Samaria, and even to the uttermost part of the earth" (Acts i. 8).

"And they were all filled with the Holy Ghost, and they began to speak with divers tongues, according as the Holy Ghost gave them to speak" (Acts ii. 4).

"And all the temptation being ended, the devil departed from Him for a time" (Luke iv. 13).

"You have not chosen Me: but I have chosen you; and have appointed you, that you should go, and should bring forth fruit; and your fruit should remain: that whatsoever you shall ask of the Father in My name, He may give it you" (John xv. 16).

"And when you fast, be not as the hypocrites, sad. For they disfigure their faces, that they may appear unto men to fast. Amen I say to you, they have received their reward" (Matt. vi. 16).

"I am the vine; you the branches: he that abideth in Me, and I in him, the same beareth much fruit: for without Me you can do nothing" (John xv. 5).

"He said, therefore, to them again: Peace be to you. As the Father hath sent Me, I also send you.

When He had said this, He breathed on them; and He said to them: Receive ye the Holy Ghost.

Whose sins you shall forgive, they are forgiven them; and whose *sins* you shall retain, they are retained" (John xx. 21–23).

"When, therefore, they had dined, Jesus saith to Simon Peter: Simon, son of John, lovest thou Me more than these?

He saith to Him: Yea, Lord, Thou knowest that I love Thee. He saith to him: Feed My lambs.

He saith to him again: Simon, *son* of John, lovest thou Me? He saith to Him: Yea, Lord, Thou knowest that I love Thee. He saith to him: Feed My lambs.

He said to him the third time: Simon, son of John, lovest thou Me? Peter was grieved, because He had said to him the third time: Lovest thou Me? And he said to Him: Lord, Thou knowest all things: Thou knowest that I love Thee. He said to him: Feed My sheep" (John xxi. 15–17).

"Jesus saith to them: But Whom do you say that I am?

Simon Peter answered and said: Thou art Christ, the Son of the living God.

And Jesus answering, said to him: Blessed art thou, Simon Bar-Jona: because flesh and blood hath not revealed it to thee, but My Father Who is in heaven.

And I say to thee: That thou art Peter; and upon this rock I will build My Church, and the gates of hell shall not prevail against it.

And I will give to thee the keys of the kingdom of heaven. And whatsoever thou shalt bind upon earth, it shall be bound also in heaven: And whatsoever thou shalt loose on earth, it shall be loosed also in heaven" (Matt. xvi. 15–19).

Activities

The stories of the Old Testament offer excellent opportunities for spontaneous dramatization in the classroom, and for a more formal literary dramatization. Suggestions are contained in *Practical Aids for Catholic Teachers* by Sister Aurelia and Father Kirsch (pp. 234–238). Suggestive dramatizations are offered (pp. 242–245) of:

Adoration of the Shepherd
Adoration of the Magi
Jesus Blessing Little Children
St. Francis and the Wolf

St. Francis Preaching to the Birds
Blessed Herman Joseph and the Infant Jesus
Pantomime — Blessed Herman Joseph*

The student will prepare a booklet on his patron saint in this grade. He will also prepare one on some major saint, presenting orally to the class, toward the end of the semester or year, a summary of what he learned. Sand-table projects, posters, calendars, booklets, plays, stories, collection of poems, pictures, even movies, furnish fresh methods of approach, or methods of reënforcing more conventional methods of learning.

Pictures

The texts in this grade both basal and supplementary will have good pictures. Special attention is called to the pictures by Gibhard Fügel in a German school bible, *Bergmann's Katholische Schulbibel*, (Muller). The following pictures with others, besides being valuable in themselves, will serve as an additional interest for the topics of the grade:

St. John and the Virgin Mary — Plockhorst
St. John Evangelist — Correggio
Sistine Madonna — Raphael
Madonna of the Chair — Raphael
Mater Dolorosa — Guido Reni
Madonna in Adoration — Correggio
Immaculate Conception — Murillo
Coronation of the Virgin — Fra Angelico
Christ Washing Peter's Feet — Ford Brown
Denial of St. Peter — Harrack

---

*The steps in analyzing a story either in preparation for a dramatization or for writing a biography are illustrated in the article by Miss Margaret Canty, entitled "Joseph the Dreamer," published in the March, 1931, issue of the CATHOLIC SCHOOL JOURNAL.

The Ascension — Hoffmann
St. John and St. Peter — Durer
St. Peter Walking on the Sea — Giotto
St. Peter in Prison — Raphael
Deliverance of St. Peter — Lippi
Crucifixion of St. Peter — Lippi
Martyrdom of St. Stephen — Fra Angelico
St. Mark Rescuing a Slave — Tintoretto
Christian Martyrs — Gerome
Paul Shipwrecked — Doré
St. Paul and St. Mark — Durer
Apparition of the Cross to Constantine — Pupils of Raphael
Victory of Constantine the Great over Maxentius
Descent from the Cross — Rubens
Crucifixion — Martini
Christ Bearing His Cross — Hoffmann
Last Communion of St. Jerome — Damenichino
Madonna with St. Jerome — Correggio
Vision of St. Augustine — Botticelli
Sir Galahad — Watts
Tapestry Weavers — Velasques
Jesus Healing the Ten Lepers — Edwin Long
Cathedral of Rheims
Tomb of Dante
Cathedral of Milan
St. Anthony of Padua — Murrillo
Poverty — Giotto
Group of Monks — Pinturicchio
St. Peter's, Rome
Francis Xavier
The Communicants
Pope Pius X
The Last Supper — Da Vinci

Religious Vocabulary

Special care must be taken to see that the child's
religious vocabulary is increased in connection partic-

ularly with the main topic of the grade, and that the new words are taught as the need develops and in the actual situation. Care should be taken to review words previously learned and to be sure a correct meaning is given to them on the child's own level. The words should grow in connotation as his religious knowledge and experience increases. Words that will generally be taught in this grade are:

emperor	Mahometan	conception
apostles	infidels	ascension
converts	saints	resurrection
pagans	universities	baptized
Constantine	apostacy	martyrs
doctrines	Jesuits	heretics
monks	hospitals	cathedral
barbarians	Vatican	monastic
monasteries	doctors	crusades
Mohammedans	crucify	Lepanto
chivalry	Holy Ghost	immaculate
indulgences	martyrdom	atrocities
vows	council	religious orders
missionaries	patriarch	Franciscans
Dominicans	migration	reign of terror
sects	schism	concordat
infallibility		

Each teacher will be required to make up her specific lists for her specific children. No stress need be placed on the spelling of these words. They may be left on the board for reference.

Poems

The poems suggested for the fifth grade carrying along the fundamental idea of the curriculum and furnishing reënforcement for the central interest of this grade are:

Christmas Night — Rev. Frederick W. Faber
The Lamb
They of the East Beheld the Star — John Pierpont
The Chapel in the Woods — Denis A. McCarthy
The Annunciation — Adelaide Anne Procter
The Mother's Quest — Rev. Hugh Francis Blunt
A Legend
Guardian Angel — Cardinal Newman
Franciscan Aspiration — Vachel Lindsay
Martyrdom of Father Campion — Henry Walpole, Jesuit
The Man of the House — Katherine Tynan Hinkson
Father Damien
The Child of Mary's Prayer — Rev. Frederick C. Kolbe, D.D.
My God, I Love Thee — St. Francis Xavier
Hymn to Saint La Salle — Mercedes
The Song of the Creatures — St. Francis of Assisi
Little Jesus — Francis Thompson
The Basque Song — Anon. trans. from the Basque
Saint Anthony of Padua — Robert Hugh Benson
Tradition — Father Tabb
Trees — Joyce Kilmer
The Martyred Saints — From the Roman Breviary, p. 420
Peter — Whatever Thou Shalt Bind on Earth — From the Roman Breviary
The Lord Commands; and Lo, His Iron Chains — From the Roman Breviary
St. Stephen, The First Martyr — Aubrey De Vere
Child of Mary
Mary Immaculate — Eleanor C. Donnelly
Pure, Meek, With Soul Serene — Roman Breviary
Truth — Horatius Bonar
Breaking a Habit — John Boyle O'Reilly
Power Made Perfect in Infirmity — Eleanor C. Donnelly
Content and Rich — Rev. R. Southwell, S.J.
Prayer for Rising — Lady Georgiana Fullerton
By Degrees — J. C. Holland
God in the Night — Rev. Abram J. Ryan
The Thought of God — Rev. Frederick W. Faber

Not Myrrh nor Frankincense I Bring — Rev. Francis J. Butler
Beauty in Common Things — Minot J. Savage
Our Birth — William Wordsworth
A Prayer — Edwin Markham
Be What Thou Seemest
Lucy's Rosary — J. R. Marre
Lead, Kindly Light — Cardinal Newman
Labor
Our Life is but a Little Holding, Lent — George Meredith
The Power of God — Thomas Moore
When Evening Shades are Falling — Thomas Moore
The Bluebird — Father Tabb
The Precious Blood of Jesus — Henry Coyle
St. Joseph's Month — H. W.
Proud Boast — Sister M. Madeleva
To a Holy Innocent — Edward F. Garesché, S.J.
Old Nuns — James M. Hayes

Additional poems should be used emphasizing the public life of Christ which is the center of interest in this grade. Children should be encouraged to "learn by heart" as many poems as possible. All should be required to learn some; many of the poems should be left to the student's own taste. The more difficult poems will be read to the class by the teachers; some poems will be read for their general idea without detailed study, and some poems will be studied in detail. Poems dealing with the same subject in earlier grades should be recalled to mind after the first reading of new poems. The poems suggested above, with others, are included in *Religious Poems for Children, Intermediate Grades*. (Bruce.)

Aspirations, Brief Prayers, Meditations

As opportunity offers, the following aspirations or others will be taught. One might be selected and written on the board each month, calling attention to it as opportunity permits. The students might prepare aspirations of their own. We inserted the tenth one on our list as suggestive of others, too, to furnish a basis for the beginning of the practice of meditation.

1. O sweetest Heart of Jesus, I implore that I may ever love Thee more and more.
2. O Mary conceived without sin, pray for us who have recourse to thee.
3. Inflame our hearts with the fire of the Holy Spirit that we may serve Thee with chaste bodies and please Thee with clean hearts.
4. Blessed be the Holy and Immaculate Conception of the Blessed Virgin Mary.
5. Mother of Love, of Sorrow, and of Mercy, pray for us.
6. Savior of the world, have mercy on us.
7. Jesus, my God, I love Thee above all things.
8. Sweet Jesus, be not to me a Judge but a Savior.
9. Holy Spirit, enlighten me.
10. What doth it profit a man if he gain the whole world but suffer the loss of his own soul.

Prayers

As the child develops, the form of prayers he will learn will change. The form of morning prayer will undoubtedly change from the simplest form to the use of the liturgical prayers of the Church. This will be generally the development. There will be, of course, an increase in the number of prayers, so that by the end of the elementary school the student will be acquainted with the principal prayers of the Church.

1. Morning prayers
2. Evening prayers
3. Grace before meals
4. Grace after meals
5. Act of Contrition
6. Act of Faith
7. Act of Hope
8. Act of Charity
9. Stations of the Cross
10. The Gloria
11. Prayers of thanksgiving and praise from the Psalms
12. The Confiteor
13. Litany of the Saints
14. Prayer before a Crucifix

Hymns

Hymns are an important factor in reënforcing the general religious instruction and training, valuable for their own content, and, if properly taught, add an element of joy in religious instruction that is quite important. The child should, at the end of instruction, know the great hymns of the Church. For the fifth grade, there is suggested the following to be sung within the voice range of the children:

1. To Christ the King
2. O Sanctissima
3. Holy Patron Thee Saluting
4. Hail, Aloysius, Hail
5. Hail, Glorious St. Patrick
6. Carmel's Little Flower

7. Out of the Depths (De Profundis)
8. Fuel in the Panting Heart of Rome

Liturgy

In this grade the liturgical vessels and utensils will be studied: The consecrated paten and chalice, the blessed ciborium, lunette, and monstrance, and the thurible or censer, the sanctus bell, the processional cross. This study of the liturgical vessels and utensils will be supplemented by the name and use of the principal liturgical linen. The child should be shown both the vessels and the linen in their actual place on the altar by the priest or assistant using the opportunity for further instruction.

Useful supplementary material for the study of various aspects of the liturgy will be found in Father Dunney's *The Mass* (Macmillan), and Father M. S. MacMahon's *Liturgical Catechism* (Gill & Son, Dublin), and *St. Andrew's Missal.*

Religious Information

There are certain facts about religious persons, vestments, ceremonies, and institutions that are a part of the equipment of every cultivated person, as well as essential, or at least supplementary, to religious practice. These need to be taught, and specific provision should be made for the instruction.

One is surprised often to find adults who do not know what INRI means, or *Alpha* and *Omega*, or even IHS, why the Mass is said in Latin, or who some prominent character in the Old or New Testament is. The teacher should use every opportunity to give such information whenever she discovers there is need for it. In this grade will be taught, in addition to what the teacher discovers to be the need of the pupil, the following:

Geography of Palestine in Christ's Day

A. Main divisions of Palestine
  1. Judea, Samaria, Galilee, Perea
B. Principal Places
  1. Bethlehem, Nazareth
  2. Jerusalem
  3. Bethsaida, Capharnaum, Cana
  4. Damascus
C. The Dead Sea, the Sea of Galilee, and River Jordan
D. Detailed Study of Jerusalem
  1. Gethsemane
  2. Mount of Olives
  3. The Gates
  4. Via Dolorosa
  5. Calvary
E. Practice in Map Drawing

Facts About New Testament

A. Language of the New Testament
B. Jewish Life in Christ's Day
  1. The Principal Sects
    a) Pharisees
    b) Sadducees
C. Official Life
  1. The Scribes
  2. The Sanhedrin
  3. Synagogue
  4. Tribute money

5. The Publicans

D. Historical Background

   1. The Roman Empire

Volume IV of Father Hugh Pope's *The Catholic Student's Aids to the Study of the Bible* (second edition, revised) is an authoritative and valuable source of information in the New Testament generally and the Gospels. Its outline will be generally useful.

A specially useful source of questions and answers for this part of the course on religious information is Father John F. Sullivan's *Externals of the Catholic Church, Her Government, Ceremonies, Festivals, Sacramentals and Devotions* (Kenedy), and Father Conway's *The Question Box*. The new *Catholic Dictionary* is specially useful. For reference the *Catholic Encyclopedia* is indispensable.

This heading is placed in the curriculum so that the teacher will realize the relative importance of this informational background to the main purpose, and will not give it undue emphasis at the expense of weightier matters. Information should be given as information.

Religious Practice

A definite part of the program in every grade is to build up the practice of religion in every grade and have the development cumulative throughout the grades. Wherever teachers see opportunity to build up Catholic practice they should do so. Teachers must not confound the lessons that may be essential and the actual practice in the life of the child. The pupil should understand the importance of interior disposition.

In the assignment to grade, the purpose is to provide

a specific time to see that the practice is established and understood. In some cases the habit will have been established. The cumulative listing of these practices is to emphasize the fact that they are not taught or established once and you are through with them. The practice must continue to be stimulated until it is "securely rooted in the life of the individual."

There should be emphasized in this grade:

1. Morning Prayer
2. Evening Prayer
3. Regular attendance at Mass on Sundays
4. Attendance at Mass on all holydays of obligation
5. Angelus
6. Bowing at the name of Jesus
7. Tipping hat or bowing as one passes a Catholic church
8. Tipping hat when one meets a Priest or Sister or other religious
9. Monthly Communion or more frequently
10. Keeping spirit of Lent by sacrifice
11. Saying Stations of the Cross
12. Practice of saying brief prayers or ejaculations or aspirations in time of temptation
13. Prayer for our parents

Practical Life

The translation of the religious knowledge, practice, and attitudes in the day-to-day life of the child must always be an objective in religious education. The elevation of the actual daily life of the individual to a supernatural plane will come about through the character of the individual's motivation. This must be a matter of development; the child must be taken, however, where he is. The lines of development are indicated, but the more specific content is left for the experimentation of the first year. A teacher should always take advantage of any actual situation, and should always strive to meet difficulties which her children, as a group, are confronted with, no matter whether it is included in the course of study or not.

1. Do a good turn every day for the love of God.
   a) Daily examination of conscience at night.
   b) Daily specific review of day's thoughts, words, or deeds.
   c) Weekly complete examination of conscience for confession or as a preparation for spiritual Communion.
   d) Daily expiation for the temporal punishment due to sin.
2. Cultivation of virtuous life.
3. Cultivation of school virtues.
4. Promotion of corporal and spiritual works of mercy.

Special attention is directed to the chapters on "The Christian Rule of Life" and "The Christian Daily Exercise" of the *Catechism of Christian Doctrine* approved by the Cardinal, Archbishops, and Bishops of England and Wales, and directed to be used in all their dioceses.

Christian Doctrine

In this grade the character of the Church, as the Body of Christ, its marks, and attributes are studied in their historical setting. Typical saints are studied in each century, and the fuller significance of the Communion of Saints, the deposit of grace, and the doctrine of indulgences is indicated. The power of the Church to teach and command is noted, as are the particular precepts of the Church that are noted for special attention.

Texts and Teaching Material

An adequate basal text on the New Testament on the fifth-grade level is not now available. The syllabus contains the detailed outline of the instruction. It is expected that the experience of the first year will give an adequate basis for a text especially prepared for the course written with a biographical emphasis. The following newer texts may prove useful:

Bible Stories for Children — Sister Anna Louise
Bible History of the Old and New Testament with Compendium of Church History — Sister Anna Louise
Compendium of Bible and Church History — Brother Eugene
Important Events in Church History — Brother Eugene
Illustrated Bible History — Rev. Ignatius Schuster
A Child's Garden of Religion Stories — Rev. P. Henry Matimore
Wonder Stories of God's People — Rev. P. Henry Matimore
A Rhymed Alphabet of Saints — Father Benson, Reginald Balfane, and S. C. Ritchies, (Benziger)[1]
Little Lives of the Saints for Children — Th. Berthold's (Benziger)
Catholic Truth Society *Catholic Biographies*, 8 vols. (Herder)

Valuable suggestions may be secured from stories in school readers. A partial list indicating the range as

---

[1]All students should own a copy of this. It might be memorized in whole or in part.

well as technique of the material is given at the end of this grade.

LIVES OF THE SAINTS IN SCHOOL READERS

It might prove suggestive as to method if the existing material in some of the readers regarding the saints were listed so that it might be consulted. Teachers should be careful to watch what is included in other subjects in a grade, so that it can be corrected or related to the work in religion. The material* is as follows:

Where Name of Author is Given

Benson, Robert Hugh
St. Anthony of Padua	Marquette	One
St. Anthony of Padua	Misericordia	Three
St. Christopher	Misericordia	Three

Berington, Rev. Joseph
St. Bernard	Catholic National	Six

Bridgett, Rev. T. E., C.S.S.R.
Martyrdom of Bl. John Fisher	Standard Catholic	Five

Christie, Rev. A. J.
The Judgment of St. Cecilia	Catholic National	Six

Coyle, Henry
St. Anne De Beaupre	Standard Catholic	Six

De Vere, Aubrey
St. Stephen, the First Martyr	Ideal Reader	Five
St. Brigid and the Blind Nun	De La Salle	Six
St. Leo the Great	Literature and Art	Six

Donnelly, Eleanor C.
Pancratius	Catholic National	Five

---

*Part of a bachelor's thesis at Marquette University by Sr. M. Leocadia analyzing the religious contents of Catholic and non-Catholic readers.

St. Patrick at Tara	Ideal Reader	Five
Egan, Maurice Francis		
St. Joan of Arc	Corona Reader	Three
Hemans, Felicia D.		
Joan of Arc at Rheims	Standard Catholic	Six
Hobart, Sarah D.		
The Legend of St. Frida	Literature and Art	Four
Jordan, Margaret E.		
St. Catherine of Siena	Literature and Art	Five
Kingsley, Charles		
St. Elizabeth's Song	Literature and Art	Five
Leo, Brother		
The Boyhood of a Saint	Cathedral Reader	Six
Lingard, Rev. John		
Venerable Joan of Arc	Catholic National	Five
Longfellow, Henry W.		
The Sermon of St. Francis	De La Salle	Five
McCarthy, Denis A.		
St. Patrick and the Shamrock	Corona Reader	Four
St. Lucy	Corona Reader	Four
St. Brigid	Cathedral Reader	Five
St. Agnes of Rome	Corona Reader	Six
Mercedes		
Hymn to St. La Salle	De La Salle	Five
Mullaney, Rev. Leo J.		
St. Ignatius Loyola	Cathedral Reader	Five
Newman, John Henry		
St. Pius V and the Battle of Lepanto	Catholic National	Six
St. Philip in His School	Literature and Art	Six
O'Reilly, Rev. A. J.		
The Last Martyr of the Coliseum	Catholic National	Six
Sadlier, Anna T.		
St. Bridget	Literature and Art	Five
Sangster, Margaret E.		
St. Martin and the Beggar	Literature and Art	Four
Skidmore, Harriet M.		
The Rock of St. Peter	Catholic National	Six
The Rock of St. Peter	De La Salle	Six

Southey, Robert
    Joan of Arc | Catholic National | Six

Southey, Robert		
Joan of Arc	Catholic National	Six
Starr, Eliza Allen		
St. Catherine of Alexandria	Literature and Art	Four
St. Sebastian	Catholic National	Six
Stewart, Agnes		
Sentence of Sir Thomas More	Catholic National	Six
Tennyson, Alfred		
St. Agnes' Eve	Ideal Reader	Six
Tynan, Katherine Hinkson		
St. Francis and The Wolf	Cathedral Reader	Six
Vaughan, Very Rev. Prior		
St. Thomas of Aquino	Catholic National	Six
Ward, S.		
St. Cecilia of Upper Peter	Ideal Reader	Five
Whittier, J. G.		
St. Patrick	Corona Reader	Four

Anonymous Selections

St. Agnes	Ideal	One
Blessed Herman Joseph	Marquette	One
St. Joseph	Marquette	One
St. Francis	Cathedral	Two
St. Gerard	Misericordia	One
St. Francis and The Wolf	Misericordia	One
Blessed Herman Joseph	Misericordia	Two
St. Felix and The Spider	Misericordia	Two
Blessed Imelda's First Communion	Misericordia	Two
Tarsicius	Misericordia	Two
St. Anthony	Misericordia	Three
The Little Flower of Jesus	Misericordia	Three
St. Blaise	Misericordia	Three
St. Christopher	Misericordia	Three
St. Joseph	Literature and Art	Two
St. Agnes — Roman Maiden	Literature and Art	Two
Blessed Imelda	Literature and Art	Two
St Elizabeth	Literature and Art	Two

St. Francis and The Birds	Marquette	Two
St. Elizabeth	Marquette	Two
St. Jerome and The Lion	Marquette	Two
St. Christopher	Marquette	Two
Brother Joseph's Mistake	Rosary	Two
The String of Beads	Rosary	Two
The Scarlet Cloak	Rosary	Two
How Jesus Came	Rosary	Two
The Pet of Gubbio	Rosary	Two
Flowers for St. Joseph	Rosary	Two
Legend of Little Herman	Standard Catholic	Two
Bernadette of Lourdes	American	Three
The Lily of The Indians	American	Three
The Poor Little One	American	Three
St. Christopher	American	Three
Finding a Way to Heaven	American	Three
St. Valentine	Cathedral	Three
St. Agnes	Cathedral	Three
Our Dumb Friends	Catholic National	Three
St. Christopher	Catholic National	Three
St. Elizabeth	Catholic National	Three
St. Germaine	Catholic National	Three
St. Peter Claver	Catholic National	Three
St. Francis of Assisi	Corona	Three
Aloysius, the Boy Saint	Corona	Three
St. Rose of Lima	Corona	Three
St. Theresa	Corona	Three
St. Cecilia	Standard Catholic	Three
St. Rose of Lima	Standard Catholic	Three
St. Anthony of Padua	Standard Catholic	Three
St. Francis of Assisi	Standard Catholic	Three
St. Veronica and The Kerchief	Standard Catholic	Three
St. Valentine's Day	Standard Catholic	Three
Joan of Arc	Standard Catholic	Three
St. Patrick	Standard Catholic	Three
St. Phocas	Standard Catholic	Three
St. Anthony	Literature and Art	Three

St. Gudula	Literature and Art	Three
St. Phocas, the Gardener	Literature and Art	Three
St. Sebastian, the Soldier	Literature and Art	Three
St. Cecilia	Literature and Art	Three
St. Rose of Lima	Cathedral	Four
St. Aloysius	Cathedral	Four
St. Agnes	Catholic National	Four
Father Isaac Jogues	Catholic National	Four
St. Patrick	Corona	Four
Martyrdom of Pancratius	Corona	Four
St. Francis Xavier	Corona	Four
St. Genevieve	Corona	Four
St. Cyril, Child-Martyr	De La Salle	Four
St. Felicitas and Her Sons	De La Salle	Four
St. John Baptist De La Salle	De La Salle	Four
St. John, The Baptist	Ideal Reader	Four
St. Joseph and The Orphan	Ideal Reader	Four
The First Martyr	Ideal Reader	Four
St. Jerome and The Lion	Literature and Art	Four
St. Macarius and The Grapes	Literature and Art	Four
St. Christopher	Literature and Art	Four
Blessed Thomas More	Literature and Art	Four
St. Francis and The Doves	Literature and Art	Four
St. Paul	Literature and Art	Four
St. Elizabeth	Standard Catholic	Four
St. Joseph, Friend of Children	Standard Catholic	Four
St. Martin's Cloak	Standard Catholic	Four
St. Cecilia — a Martyr	Catholic National	Five
St. Tarsicius	De La Salle	Five
St. Dorothy, Martyr	De La Salle	Five
St. Philip Neri	De La Salle	Five
Pancratius, The Martyr's Boy	De La Salle	Five
St. Rose of Lima	Ideal	Five
St. Philip Neri	Literature and Art	Five
St. Francis and The Birds	Standard Catholic	Five
St. Charles Borromeo	Catholic National	Six
Martyrdom of Pancratius	De La Salle	Six

St. Agnes and Fulvius	De La Salle	Six
St. Vincent de Paul	Ideal	Six
The Martyr's Boy	Ideal	Six
St. George	Literature and Art	Six
St. Mark at The Moon-gate	Literature and Art	Six
St. Joan of Arc	Standard Catholic	Six
St. Augustine and The English	Standard Catholic	Six

RELIGION IN GRADE VI

Main Interest: The Mass

THE center of interest in the sixth grade is the Mass. This will begin with a review of the elements already presented in earlier grades. The emphasis in this grade will be the unchanging parts of the Mass; i.e., the Ordinary of the Mass. Those parts of the Mass that vary will be followed throughout the liturgical year in the seventh and eighth grades. A beginning of this will be made in this grade.

Outline of Main Topics

I. *The sacrifices in the Old Law*
II. *Christ's Passion, Death, Resurrection, and Ascension*
III. *The new priesthood (sacrament of holy orders)*
IV. *Review of the establishment of the Holy Eucharist*
V. *The preparation for baptism in the early Church*
VI. *The Mass of the Catechumens*
    1. Prayers at the foot of altar
    2. Introit
    3. Kyrie, eleison
    4. Gloria in excelsis
    5. Collect
    6. Commemoration, if any
    7. Epistle
    8. Gradual, Sequence, Tract, and Alleluia

9. Gospel
10. Creed

VII. *The Mass of the Faithful*

1. Offertory — offering of Host
2. Oblation prayers — offering of Chalice
3. Lavabo
4. Secrets
5. Preface
6. Sanctus
7. Canon of the Mass
   a) Commemoration of living
   b) Communicantes
   c) Consecration of the Host
   d) Elevation of the Host
   e) Consecration of the Chalice
   f) Elevation of the Chalice
   g) Commemoration of the Dead
8. Pater Noster
9. Communion
10. Postcommunion
11. Ite Missa Est
12. Last Gospel

VIII. *Parts of Mass that do not change*

1. Prayers at foot of altar
2. Kyrie, eleison
3. Gloria (when said)
4. Credo (when said)
5. Oblation prayers
6. Canon
7. Pater Noster
8. Ite Missa (when said)
9. Last Gospel (when said)

IX. *Parts of the Mass sometimes omitted*
1. Gloria
2. Gradual, Tract, Sequence, and Alleluia
3. Creed
4. Ite Missa Est
X. *Teach the Latin keywords for changes in the Mass*

Quotations

The quotations studied in this grade are a reënforcement and development of the material included in the second grade. All quotations in the second grade will be especially reviewed, and those in the fifth grade will be recalled, and the following additional ones will be used as the outline develops.

"And whilst they were at supper, Jesus took bread, and blessed, and broke: and gave to His disciples, and said: Take ye, and eat. This is My Body.

"And taking the chalice, He gave thanks, and gave to them, saying: Drink ye all of this.

"For this is My Blood of the New Testament, which shall be shed for many unto remission of sins" (Matt. xxvi. 26–28).

"And taking bread, He gave thanks, and brake; and gave to them, saying: This is My Body, which is given for you. Do this for a commemoration of Me" (Luke xxii. 19).

"For I have received of the Lord that which also I delivered unto you, that the Lord Jesus, the same night in which He was betrayed, took bread.

"And giving thanks, broke, and said: Take ye, and eat: This is My Body, which shall be delivered for you: this do for the commemoration of Me.

"In like manner also the chalice, after He had supped, saying: This chalice is the New Testament in My Blood: this do ye, as often as you shall drink, for the commemoration of Me.

"For as often as you shall eat this Bread, and drink the Chalice, you shall shew the death of the Lord, until He come.

"Therefore whosoever shall eat this Bread, or drink the Chalice of the Lord unworthily, shall be guilty of the Body and of the Blood of the Lord.

"But let a man prove himself: and so let him eat of that Bread, and drink of the Chalice" (I Cor. xi. 23–28).

"Jesus saith to her: Woman, believe Me, that the hour cometh, when you shall neither on this mountain, nor in Jerusalem, adore the Father . . .

"But the hour cometh, and now is, when the true adorers shall adore the Father in spirit and in truth. For the Father also seeketh such to adore Him" (John iv. 21, 23).

"Jesus answered, and said to her: Whosoever drinketh of this water, shall thirst again, but he that shall drink of the water that I will give him, shall not thirst for ever" (John iv. 13).

"And the centurion making answer, said: Lord, I am not worthy that Thou shouldst enter under my roof: but only say the word, and my servant shall be healed" (Matt. viii. 8).

"Jesus said to her: I am the Resurrection and the Life: he that believeth in Me, although he be dead, shall live" (John xi. 25).

Activities

The most obvious supplementary activity for the work of the sixth grade would be the preparation of a *Mass Book* for the student which would include among other things:

The name and source of the vestments worn by the priest.

The institution of the Holy Eucharist.

The parts of the Mass classified in various ways.

The various kinds of Masses.

The part of the laity in the Mass.

The *Mass Book* will be made up of pictures selected from various sources, of historical notes regarding the Mass, of diagrams and charts, and the practical devotional aspects of the Mass.

A notation might be made on the Masses of each Sunday and holyday of obligation. The calendar in the CATHOLIC SCHOOL JOURNAL each month during the school year, 1930–31, might be suggestive in connection with this last part of the project. The notations in the *St. Andrew's Missal* will also be very helpful. The pamphlets called *With Mother Church* (Books 1, 2, 3, 4) might furnish suggestions for the making of this *Mass Book*.

Pictures

The pictures that should be used to reënforce the main topic of the sixth grade are the lantern slides and stereographs of Father George A. Keith, S.J., of Loyola University, Chicago. These may be secured from the Keystone View Company, Meadville, Pa.

It would be worth while for the enthusiasm it would create to have Father Keith personally present his material to the sixth-grade children of a city in the morning and to the parent-teacher associations in the evening.

Religious Vocabulary

Special care must be taken to see that the child's religious vocabulary is increased in connection particularly with the main topic of the grade, and that the new words are taught as the need develops and in the actual situation. Care should be taken to review words previously learned and to be sure a correct meaning is given to them on the child's own level. The words should grow in connotation as his religious knowledge and experience increases. This gradual vocabulary acquisition will prove lasting.

Words that will generally be taught in this grade are:

absolution	eternal	Offertory
begotten	everlasting	paten
Canon	faith	redemption
Communion	Gospel	remembrance
Consecration	humanity	remission
consubstantial	intercession	salvation
creed	Introit	testament
divinity	mystery	venerable
elevation	oblation	vouchsafe
Epistle		

Each teacher will be required to make up her specific lists for her specific children. No stress need be placed on the spelling of these words. They may be left on the board for reference.

Poems

The poems suggested for the sixth grade carrying along the fundamental idea of the curriculum and furnishing reënforcement for the central interest of this grade are:

Loneliness, Edwin Essex
The Star's Song, Father Ryan
The Lamb, William Blake
Christ and the Little Ones, Julia Gill
Discontent, Sarah Orne Jewett
How the Gates Came Ajar!
The Infant Jesus, Rev. Frederick W. Faber
Bethlehem, Phillips Brooks

The Baby
A Christmas Song, Teresa Brayton
Anointed, Hallowing Hands, Caroline C. MacGill
The Young Priest to His Hands, Edward F. Garesché, S.J.
An Old Woman's Rosary, Hugh F. Blunt
Charity, Christina Rossetti
The Rainbow, Christina Rossetti
The Rainbow, John Keble
Speak, Little Voice, Rev. M. Earls, S.J.
Mary Magdalene, Christina Rossetti
The Catechism of the Clock, Eleanor C. Donnelly
Holy Communion, Speer Strahan
Mary Magdalen, J. J. Callahan
A Sermon, Charles Mackay
After a Visit to the Blessed Sacrament, S. H. St. John
The Month of Mary, John Henry
Herself a Rose, Christina Rossetti
Our Lord and Our Lady, Hilaire Belloc
The Patronage of St. Joseph, Frederick W. Faber
His Christmas Tree, Rev. P. J. Carroll, C.S.C.
Easter Lilies, Rev. John B. Tabb
A Rosary Molded of Rose Leaves, Rev. C. L. O'Donnell,
 C.S.C.
The Sisters, Eleanor C. Donnelly
The Crucifixion, Montgomery
A Passage in the Life of St. Augustine, Anon.
Brigid and the Blind Nun, Aubrey de Vere
The Rock of St. Peter, Harriet M. Skidmore
A Legend, Adelaide Procter
The Eighth Psalm, The Bible
The Nativity, John Bannister Tabb
No Room in the Inn, Agnes Repplier
The Virgin, William Wordsworth
God's Presence in Nature, Thomas Moore
To the Ever Blessed Virgin, Monsignor John S. Vaughan
On Through Your Round of Duties Plod, Father Russell
Love Thy God, and Love Him Only, Aubrey De Vere
Hymn to the Virgin, Sir Walter Scott

"Come to Me," Henry Coyle
Consider the Lilies of the Field, Christina G. Rossetti
The Prayer of St. Francis Xavier, Alexander Pope
Father Damien, Rev. John B. Tabb
He Comes, Rev. Francis J. Butler
But, Above All, the Victory is Most Sure, William Wordsworth
Judge not: The Workings of His Brain, Adelaide A. Procter
Vital Spark of Heavenly Flame, Alexander Pope
My Life, Rev. John B. Tabb
The Power of God, Thomas Moore
The Lost Chord, Adelaide A. Procter
Joseph's Thoughts, Rev. E. F. Gareschè, S.J.
A Psalm of Life, Henry Wadsworth Longfellow
Thy Will Be Done, John Austin
The Mercies of God, Joseph Addison
Thankfulness, Adelaide A. Procter
Doing the Will of God, Eleanor C. Donnelly
One King Omnipotent, Samuel Johnson
In the Tomb, Rev. Hugh F. Blunt
The Real Presence, Denis A. McCarthy
Our Ambition, St. Bernard of Clairvaux
Lord! Who Thy Thousand Years Dost Wait, Cardinal Newman
The Sleep, Elizabeth Barrett Browning
The Sign of the Cross, Cardinal Newman
At Morn — At Noon — At Twilight Dim, Edgar Allan Poe
Prayer, James Montgomery
A Saintly Wish, C. F. Alexander
A Golden Rule, A Sister of Notre Dame
St. Agnes' Eve, Alfred Tennyson
Hymn to the Sacred Heart, Mercedes
One Thing Alone, Dear Lord! I Dread, Rev. F. W. Faber
Give Me, O Lord, a Heart of Grace, Lady Gilbert
Ave Maria, Sir Walter Scott
All Wait on Thee, Christina Rossetti
Divine Creator of the Light, Daniel Joseph Donahoe

My Beads, Rev. Abram J. Ryan
The Poor Man's Daily Bread, Denis A. McCarthy
A Friend, Lionel Johnson
An Old Woman of the Roads, Padraic Colum
The Glories of the World Sink Down in Gloom, Joseph
    Plunkett
The Thirteenth Station, Caroline Giltinan
An Autumn Rose-Tree, Michael Earls
The Soul of Karnaghan Buidhe, James B. Dollard
Our Lord and Our Lady, Hilaire Belloc
Consider, Christina Rossetti
Lord What Have I to Offer?, Christina Rossetti
The Hymn of the Blessed Virgin
On His Blindness, John Milton
The Sandpiper, Celia Thaxter
The Question, Rachel Annand Taylor
Communion, Caroline Giltinan
The Last Communion
Give Me Thy Heart, Adelaide Anne Procter
Our Daily Bread
To Our Lord in the Sacrament, St. Anselm
I am the Way, Alice Meynell
I See His Blood Upon the Rose, Joseph Mary Plunkett
Feast of the Sacred Heart, Father Ryan
Cardinal Manning, Aubrey de Vere
The Pillar of the Cloud, John Henry Newman
From Torrid South to Frozen North, Cardinal Wiseman
A Thought from Cardinal Newman, Matthew Russell, S.J.
For the Feast of the Immaculate Conception, Roman Breviary
Consider Well, Blessed Thomas More
To Fortune, Blessed Thomas More
Adoro Te Devote, St. Thomas Aquinas, (from the Latin by
    Dom F. Cabrol, O.S.B.)
Christ and the Leper, N. P. Willis
Prayer of a Soldier in France, Joyce Kilmer
The Rosary of My Tears, Father Ryan
Rosary, Brother Azarias

Feast of the Finding of the Holy Cross, May 3rd, Venantius
  Fortunatus
The Vision of Monk Gabriel, Eleanor C. Donnelly
What is Prayer, James Montgomery
Relics of the Saints, John Henry Newman
Christ and the Pagan, Rev. J. B. Tabb
Carthusians, Ernest Dowson

Additional poems should be used emphasizing the
public life of Christ which is the center of interest in
the grade. Children should be encouraged to "learn by
heart" as many poems as possible. All should be required to learn some: many of the poems should be
left to the student's own taste. The more difficult poems
will be read to the class by the teacher; some poems
will be read for their general idea without detailed
study, and some poems will be studied in detail. Poems
dealing with the same subject in earlier grades should
be recalled to mind after the first reading of new
poems. The poems suggested in the foregoing, with
others, are included in *Religious Poems for Children
(Intermediate Grades)* (Bruce).

Aspirations, Brief Prayers, and Meditations

As opportunity offers, the following aspirations, or
others, will be taught. One might be selected and written on the board each month, calling attention to it as
opportunity permits. The students might prepare aspirations of their own. The following selections are
taken from the Ordinary of the Mass:

1. Show us, O Lord, Thy mercy, and grant us salvation (Asperges).

2. May Almighty God have mercy upon me and,

forgiving my sins, bring me to life everlasting (Confiteor).

3. Lord, have mercy upon us (thrice),
   Christ, have mercy upon us (thrice),
   Lord, have mercy upon us (thrice) (Kyrie, eleison).

4. My Lord and my God.

5. Be mindful also, O Lord, of Thy servants and handmaids N. and N. who are gone before us, with the sign of faith, and sleep in the sleep of peace. To these, O Lord, and to all that rest in Christ, grant, we beseech Thee, a place of refreshment, light and peace, through the same Christ our Lord (Memento of Dead).

6. Lamb of God, Who takest away the sins of the world, have mercy upon us (twice).

Lamb of God, Who takest away the sins of the world, grant us peace.

7. Lord, I am not worthy that Thou shouldst enter under my roof; say but the word and my soul shall be healed.

8. May the Body and Blood of our Lord, Jesus Christ, preserve my soul to everlasting life.

9. Pray for us, O holy Mother of God, that we may be worthy of the promises of Christ.

10. May the Sacred Heart of Jesus have mercy upon us (thrice).

Prayers

As the child develops, the form of prayers he will learn will change. The form of morning prayer will undoubtedly change from the simplest form to the use of the liturgical prayers of the Church. This will be generally the development. There will be, of course, an increase in the number of prayers, so that by the end of the elementary school the student will be acquainted with the principal prayers of the Church.

1. Morning prayers
2. Evening prayers
3. Grace before meals
4. Grace after meals
5. Act of Contrition
6. Act of Faith
7. Act of Hope
8. Act of Charity
9. Stations of the Cross
10. The Gloria
11. Prayers of thanksgiving and praise from the Psalms
12. The Confiteor
13. Litany of the Saints
14. Prayer before a Crucifix
15. Praying the Mass with the Missal

To teach prayers adequately, the instructors should understand what is meant by mysticism, and its relation to theology and asceticism. For this purpose an excellent introduction is Rev. A. J. Francis Stanton's *Catholic Mysticism* (Herder). The bibliography is excellent.

Hymns

Hymns are an important factor in reënforcing the general religious instruction and training, valuable for their own content, and if properly taught, add an element of joy in religious instruction that is quite important. The child should, at the end of instruction, know the great hymns of the Church. For the sixth grade there is suggested the following to be sung within the voice range of the children:

1. Adoro Te
2. O Salutaris Hostia
3. Tantum Ergo Sacramentum
4. The Divine Praises
5. Lord, I am not Worthy
6. Veni Sancte Spiritus

Liturgy

The greatest liturgical service of the Church, the Mass, is the center of interest in this grade. In this grade the liturgy receives the greatest emphasis and is a convenient point for the summary of points presented in earlier grades, and the basis for the practice of praying the Mass with the Missal in the two subsequent grades and in their later life.

It is highly desirable that a priest should, at the altar and fully vested, actually go through the entire service of the Mass explaining each step and action as he makes it.

Useful supplementary material for the study of various aspects of the liturgy will be found in Father Dunney's *The Mass* (Macmillan Co.), and in Rev. M. S. MacMahon's *Liturgical Catechism* (Gill & Son, Dublin), and in *St. Andrew's Missal.*

Religious Information

There are certain facts about religious persons, vestments, ceremonies, and institutions that are a part of

maia

the equipment of every cultivated person, as well as essential or at least supplementary to religious practice. These need to be taught, and specific provision should be made for the instruction.

One is surprised often to find adults who do not know what INRI means, or *Alpha* and *Omega,* or even IHS, why the Mass is said in Latin, or who some prominent character in the Old or New Testament is. The teacher should use every opportunity to give such information whenever she discovers there is need for it.

In this grade will be taught, in addition to what the teacher discovers to be the need of the pupil, the following:

Divisions of Ecclesiastical Year

I. Christmas Cycle of the Incarnation
    1. Advent
    2. Christmas
    3. Time after Epiphany
II. Easter Cycle or the Redemption (depends on Easter moon. Begins between Jan. 18 and Feb. 22.)
    1. Septuagesima (3 weeks)
    2. Lent, including Passiontide
    3. Eastertide to Pentecost
    4. Time after Pentecost (24 to 28 weeks)
III. Division of the Day.
    Seven Times a Day Did I Praise Thee
    1. Lavas (Dawn)
    2. Prime (First Hour, 6 a.m.)
    3. Tierce (Third Hour, 9 a.m.)
    4. Sext (Sixth Hour, noon)
    5. None (Lunch Hour, 3 p.m.)

6. Vespers (When Star Vesper appears, 5 p.m.)
7. Compline (Night prayers)

The Missal will give this information fully enough. The teacher might have for her own reference the *St. Andrew's Daily Missal* which is particularly rich in notes.

A specially useful source of questions and answers for this part of the course on religious information is Rev. John F. Sullivan's *Externals of the Catholic Church, Her Government, Ceremonies, Festivals, Sacramentals and Devotions*, (Kenedy) and Father Conway's *The Question Box*. The new *Catholic Dictionary* is specially useful. For reference the *Catholic Encyclopedia* is indispensable.

This heading is placed in the curriculum so that the teacher will realize the relative importance of this informational background to the main purpose, and will not give it undue emphasis at the expense of weightier matters. Information should be given as information.

Religious Practice

A definite part of the program in every grade is to build up the practice of religion in every grade and have the development cumulative throughout the grades. Wherever teachers see opportunity to build up Catholic practice they should do so. Teachers must not confound the lessons that may be essential and the actual practice in the life of the child. The pupil should understand the importance of interior disposition.

In the assignment to grade the purpose is to provide a specific time to see that the practice is established and understood. In some cases the habit will have been established. The cumulative listing of these practices is to emphasize the fact that they are not taught or established once and you are through with them. The practice must continue to be stimulated until it is "securely rooted in the life of the individual." There should be emphasized in this grade:

1. Morning Prayer
2. Evening Prayer
3. Regular attendance at Mass on Sundays
4. Attendance at Mass on all holydays of obligation
5. Angelus
6. Bowing at the name of Jesus
7. Tipping hat or bowing as one passes church
8. Tipping hat when one meets Priest or Sister or other religious
9. Monthly Communion or more frequently
10. Keeping spirit of Lent by sacrifice
11. Saying Stations of Cross
12. Practice of saying brief prayers or ejaculations or aspirations in time of temptation
13. Prayer for our parents
14. Praying the Mass with Missal

Practical Life

The translation of the religious knowledge, practice, and attitudes in the day-to-day life of the child must always be an objective in religious education. The elevation of the actual daily life of the individual to a supernatural plane will come about through the character of the individual's motivation. This must be a matter of development; the child must be taken, however, where he is. The lines of development are indicated but the more specific content is left for the experimentation of the first year. A teacher should always take advantage of any actual situation, and should always strive to meet difficulties which her children as a group are confronted with, no matter whether it is included in the course of study or not.

1. Do a good turn every day for the love of God.

a) Daily examination of conscience at night.

b) Daily specific review of day's thoughts, words, and deeds.

c) Weekly complete examination of conscience for confession or as a preparation for spiritual Communion.

d) Daily expiation for the temporal punishment due to sin.

2. Cultivation of virtuous life.

3. Cultivation of school virtues.

4. Promotion of corporal and spiritual works of mercy.

Special attention is directed to the chapters on "The Christian Rule of Life" and "The Christian Daily Exercise" of the *Catechism of Christian Doctrine* approved by the Cardinal, Archbishops, and Bishops of England and Wales, and directed to be used in all their dioceses.

Christian Doctrine

In this grade the principal doctrinal interest is in the Holy Eucharist as Sacrifice and as Sacrament. The actual text of the Mass in English is used as the basis of the study. Besides the main emphasis on the Holy Sacrifice of the Mass, the Holy Eucharist as Sacrament, Confession, and Penance, the child receives considerable information and basis for his formal study of Christian doctrine in the seventh and eighth grades on the Church, grace, the sacraments, sacramentals, prayer, and the fuller meaning of Calvary, and the continuance of the Church as the Body of Christ.

Up to this point all the doctrines of the Church to be studied in the seventh and eighth years have been studied at least once, and in some cases three and four times in their historical setting, or for the practical life of the Catholic. He, therefore, approaches the study of the doctrine with considerable information in settings in which he is interested; and now its formal organization ought to prove more interesting, more significant to him, and more easily made a guide in the practical life.

Text

The text of the sixth grade is Father Cunningham's *Christ's Gift, the Mass* (Benziger), a missal arranged very conveniently for use. It will be the child's prayer book at Mass during the sixth, seventh and eighth grades. The practice begun here with the Missal will be reënforced by the stimulation and instruction of the teachers in the seventh and eighth grades.

Other valuable missals are *The Dominical Missal* (Lohmann) and *The Small Missal* (Macmillan).

RELIGION IN GRADE VII

Main Interest: Christian Doctrine

IN the seventh year the emphasis becomes more definitely doctrinal than it has in any of the preceding years, though it is not solely doctrinal. The instruction definitely provides for the study and learning of the specific questions and answers of the *Baltimore Catechism*.

Outline of Main Topics

The topics of study included in the seventh and eighth years shall be a definite organization of the material that they have learned in the more concrete situation of the preceding grades. The work of these two grades is one continuous unit. The line of division will vary with the different classes. Ordinarily, the seventh grade will end with the completion of the life of Christ. The development of topics will be orderly, each one growing out of the preceding ones, and all will be related to life. Such an orderly development is contained in the following outline:

1. God the Creator
2. The Story of the Creation
3. Adam and Eve
4. Why God made Man
5. The Commandments of God

6. The First Commandment of God
7. The Second Commandment of God
8. The Third Commandment of God
9. The Fourth Commandment of God
10. The Fifth Commandment of God
11. The Sixth and Ninth Commandments of God
12. The Seventh and Tenth Commandments of God
13. The Eighth Commandment of God
14. Sin
15. The Messiah
16. Prepare Ye the Way of the Lord
17. The Early Life of Christ
18. The Public Life of Christ: The Parables
19. The Public Life of Christ: The Miracles
20. Some Memorable Sayings of Christ
21. Christ and the Holy Eucharist
22. The Crucifixion
23. He is Risen
24. Mary, Full of Grace
25. Christ and the Apostles
26. Holy Ghost on Pentecost

Scriptural Passages of Doctrinal Significance

There are certain passages of Scripture that have a doctrinal significance or are the basis of the Church's formulation of the doctrine. These passages, some of them learned in another grade, should now be reviewed and others added, and all memorized exactly. These passages should be placed in their context by the teacher both as a help to understanding and to memory. The following list is minimum:

"Behold, a Virgin shall conceive, and bear a Son, and His Name shall be called Emmanuel" (Isa. vii. 14).

"Jesus saith to them: But Whom do you say that I am? Simon Peter answered and said: Thou art the Christ, the Son of the Living God" (Matt. xvi. 15–16).

"Thou hast the words of Eternal Life" (John vi. 69).

"I am the Living Bread which came down from heaven" (John vi. 51).

"I am the Good Shepherd" (John x. 11).

"I am the Light of the world" (John viii. 12).

"The Word was made flesh, and dwelt among us" (John i. 14).

"For I delivered unto you first of all, which I also received: How that Christ died for our sins, according to the Scriptures:

"And that He was buried, and that He rose again the third day, according to the Scriptures:

"And that He was seen by Cephas. And after that by the eleven;

"Then was He seen by more than five hundred brethren at once: of whom many remain until this present, and some are fallen asleep.

"After that, He was seen by James; then by all the Apostles; and last of all, He was seen by me, as by one born out of due time" (I Cor. xv. 3–8).

"Other foundation no man can lay, but that which is laid; which is Christ Jesus" (I Cor. iii. 11).

"Other sheep I have, that are not of this Fold: them also I must bring, and they shall hear My voice, and there shall be One Fold and One Shepherd" (John x. 16).

"Whilst they were at supper, Jesus took bread, and blessed, and broke: and gave to His disciples, and said: Take ye and eat. This is My Body. And taking the chalice He gave thanks, and gave to them, saying: Drink ye all of this. For this is My Blood of the New Testament which shall be shed for many unto remission of sins" (Matt. xxvi. 26–28).

"Jesus said: Father, forgive them, for they know not what they do" (Luke xxiii. 34).

"Jesus said to him: Amen I say to thee, this day shalt thou be with Me in Paradise" (Luke xxiii. 43).

"When Jesus, therefore, had seen His Mother and the disciple standing whom He loved, He saith to His Mother: Woman, behold thy son. After that He saith to the disciple: Behold thy Mother. And from that hour, the disciple took her to his own" (John xix. 26–27).

"From the sixth hour there was darkness over the whole earth, until the ninth hour. And about the ninth hour Jesus cried with a loud voice, saying: Eli, Eli, lamma sabacthani? that is, My God, My God, why hast Thou forsaken Me?" (Matt. xxvii. 45, 46.)

"Jesus knowing that all things were now accomplished, that the Scripture might be fulfilled, said: I thirst" (John xix. 28).

"Jesus, therefore, when He had taken the vinegar, said: It is consummated" (John xix. 30).

"Jesus crying with a loud voice said: Father, into Thy hands I commend My Spirit" (Luke xxiii. 46).

"Jesus said to her: I am the Resurrection and the Life; he that believeth in Me, although he be dead, shall live" (John xi. 25).

"Jesus saith to him: I am the Way, and the Truth, and the Life. No man cometh to the Father but by Me" (John xiv. 6).

"God so loved the world, as to give His only-begotten Son; that whosoever believeth in Him, may not perish, but may have life everlasting" (John iii. 16).

"Thomas . . . said to Him: My Lord and my God" (John xx. 28).

"This day is born to you a Savior, Who is Christ the Lord, in the city of David" (Luke ii. 11).

"Come to Me, all you that labor and are burdened, and I will refresh you" (Matt. xi. 28).

"This is Eternal Life: that they may know Thee, the only true God, and Jesus Christ, Whom Thou hast sent" (John xviii. 3).

"It is appointed unto men once to die, and after this the judgment" (Heb. ix. 27).

Practical Applications of Religion

Definite provision should be made that actual cases of life problems should be considered where there is no doubt about the application of the religious principle or doctrine. Some typical cases illustrating the Commandments are presented as samples:

1. Sue and Jane go to the fortune teller "just for fun!" The fortune teller tells Sue something which really comes to pass shortly afterward. Sue asks you what you think about it. What would you tell her? Did the girls do right by going to a fortune teller?

2. Someone sends you a chain prayer and tells you that you will be visited by some terrible calamity if you do not say it and help to circulate it. What should you do about it? What sin do you commit by believing in such things? Mention other superstitions you know about.

3. Louis wears a four-leaved clover for good luck. You laugh at him, but he says you are just as bad, for you wear a medal and believe it is going to keep you away from harm. How will you explain the difference?

4. Why should such expressions as "Cross my heart, I'm telling the truth," and "Sure as heaven," even though they are not sins, very seldom be used?

5. A little boy has followed the example of his father in cursing. When the mother corrects him, he says: "Daddy does it, why can't I?" What do you think that mother ought to do?

6. What do you think of the Holy Name Society?

7. A young man is out all Saturday night. Before returning home on Sunday morning he enters church to hear Mass. He sleeps during the greater part of the service. Has he fulfilled his obligation? What must one do to fulfill the obligation of hearing Mass on Sundays?

8. You are on your way to church on Sunday morning. You meet Lew and ask him to come along. He says he is busy finishing the garage, but that he will make up for the Mass

by going on Monday morning instead. What will you answer? He argues that one Mass is as good as another and further, that the Church has no right to tell him what to do. Answer his arguments.

9. You are on your way to Mass on Sunday. A car ahead of yours is turned over and the driver injured. If you stop to help him you will miss the only Mass there is at your church. Should you offer your help or go to Mass?

10. Since Mr. Grey owns a radio he does not go to Mass on Sunday. He says he hears Mass and a good sermon every Sunday over the radio and really gets more out of it than when he goes to church. Is he in the right?

11. Mr. Blake is a Catholic, but he does not attend Sunday Mass. He says he will work while he is young and strong and will devote a great deal of time to his soul when he is old and can no longer work. What would you tell him?

12. If mother dresses in an old-fashioned way, would you be ashamed of her when you are with your friends in a crowd?

13. What do you think of your big sister who says to mother: "Oh shucks! You're an oldtimer."

14. What are some of the jobs you can do at home to show you love your parents?

15. When mother and father are old and perhaps poor and you are grown up, what will you do for them?

16. You may not take books home from a shelf. You started a story and want to finish it, so you slip the book between your other ones and go off with it intending to return it in the morning.

17. You see your best friend go to another boy's locker and you know the school forbids this. Soon the boy discovers that his ball is gone. What would you do about it?

18. You have chicken pox but you play with the neighbor children anyway when their mother and your mother don't see you. Are you disobeying a law?

19. Some children think it is "smart" to hang on cars, to run in front of coming automobiles or trains. Are these acts sinful? (They expose themselves to fatal accidents, unnecessarily.)

20. When you cause suffering through such a foolish joke, are you obliged to pay the bills due to doctors, hospitals, etc.?

21. Ben takes you to his home for the first time and shows you his room. The walls are filled with indecent pictures. Could you judge from them what kind of companion Ben is? Would the pictures be a sure sign that he is bad or could there be another reason for his having them? What should you do in either case?

22. Jack was sitting by the window and reading. All of a sudden he caught himself in the act of daydreaming and realized that his thoughts had drifted to forbidden things. Had Jack committed a sin up to this time? What should he do now? He takes up his book and begins to read again, but finds that he cannot get rid of his evil thoughts. Can you suggest other remedies?

23. Grace's older sister wants her to go along to a dance. Grace knows that the place has a bad reputation, but her sister says that they will stay with their own group and that, after all, it's up to a girl to keep her place. Do you think Grace should go?

24. Elsie has a new dress. She asks you how you like it. You do not like it at all, but do not wish to hurt her feelings. How would you answer her?

25. A boy asks you where you are going. You tell him you are going to the North Pole. Is that a lie?

26. You have a chance to look into your book during examination. May you do so?

27. Sometimes groups of boys or girls talk indecently. You don't want that to continue. How will you try to stop it?

Religious Vocabulary

Many of the words listed for the seventh and eighth grades have been previously met and studied in their context in earlier grades. The words have been definitely associated with ideas, and have been given in connection with concrete situations or specific explanations. In these grades in connection with the more formal teaching of doctrine and the more exact formulation of Christian doctrine, there should be a check-up of the religious vocabulary in connection with a more formal word study. The words should be studied whenever the first opportunity in these grades presents itself, wherever the word is assigned. A tentative listing of the words used in the formulation of Christian doctrine is given here:

creator	original	contempt
free will	mortal	respect
worship	consent	false witness
creed	reverence	despair
crucified	vow	relics
Trinity	Sunday	profane
mystery	confirmed	incarnation
spiritual	medium	Bethlehem
damnation	spiritists	Passion
Apostles	infidels	tidings
crucifix	presumption	Limbo
graven	brethren	Pentecost
obligation	blasphemy	covetousness
magistrates	spirit	reflection
immodesty	everlasting	sloth
ill-gotten	Catholic	oath
slander	conceived	Sabbath
impure	infinitely	adultery
memorials	divine	charms
cursing	corruption	attributing
Redeemer	venial	heretics
Annunciation	gluttony	profession
Ascension	commemoration	back-biting
sepulchre	salvation	images
scourging	worship	representation
immortal	servile	

Poems

The poems suggested for the seventh grade carrying along the fundamental idea of the curriculum and furnishing reënforcement for the central interest of this grade are:

To My God-Child, Francis Thompson
"Ex Ore Infantium," Francis Thompson
To a Snowflake, Francis Thompson
To Keep a True Lent, Robert Herrick
There's a Wideness in God's Mercy, Father Faber
Saint Peter, Aubrey De Vere
Faith, Father Faber
All of It, Rev. Hugh Francis Blunt
The Transfiguration, James H. Hayes
As Little Children, William V. Doyle, S.J.
Christ and the Pagan, John B. Tabb
To the Blessed Virgin, Wordsworth
Saint Cecilia, John Dryden
To the Blessed Virgin, Gerald Griffin
O Blessed Trinity, Father Faber
The Names of Our Lady, Adelaide A. Procter
Mary's Intercession, Sister M. Stanislaus MacCarthy, O.S.B.
Rosary, Brother Azarias
The Bells of Santa Ysabel, Mary F. Nixon-Roulet
Beautiful Mother, We Deck Thy Shrine, Rev. K. D. Beste
A Purpose of Amendment, Helen Parry Eden
The Folded Flock, Wilfrid Meynell
Wishes for My Son, Thomas MacDonagh
The Housewife's Prayer, Blanche Mary Kelly
Heaven — Heaven, Gerard Manley Hopkins
To a Martyr, Edward F. Garesché
The Cherub-Folk, Enid Dinnis
Requiescat, Oscar Wilde
Ireland, Dora Sigerson Shorter
Self-Control, John Henry Newman
Before the Ending of the Day, trans. J. M. Neale

O Christ, Whose Glory Fills the Heaven, trans. John Julian
O God, Whose Hand Hath Spread the Sky, trans. J. M. Neale
As Fades the Glowing Orb of Day, trans. Father Potter
Hail, O Queen of Heaven, Enthroned! trans. Father Caswall

Additional poems should be used emphasizing the center of interest in the grade. Children should be encouraged to "learn by heart" as many poems as possible. All should be required to learn some: many of the poems should be left to the student's own taste.

The more difficult poems will be read to the class by the teacher; some poems will be read for their general idea without detailed study, and some poems will be studied in detail. Poems dealing with the same subject in earlier grades should be recalled to mind after the first reading of new poems. The poems suggested above, with others, are included in *Religious Poems for Children (Junior-High Grades)* (Bruce).

Aspirations, Brief Prayers, and Meditations

As opportunity offers, the following aspirations or others will be taught. One might be selected and written on the board each month, calling attention to it as opportunity permits. The students might prepare aspirations of their own. The following aspirations are suggested:

1. My God, I love Thee above all things.

2. Purify, O Lord, my heart, enlighten my understanding, animate my will.

3. Inflame our hearts with the fire of the Holy Spirit that we may serve Thee with chaste bodies, and please Thee with clean hearts.

4. We adore Thee, O most blessed Lord, Jesus Christ,

we bless Thee, because by Thy holy cross Thou hast redeemed the world.

5. My God, unite all minds in the truth and all hearts in charity.

6. Mother of Love, of Sorrow, and of Mercy, pray for us.

7. Jesus, Mary, and Joseph, I give You my heart and my soul.

8. Sweet Jesus, be not to me a Judge, but a Savior.

9. Come Holy Ghost, fill the hearts of Thy faithful, and kindle in them the fire of Thy divine Love.

10. And now, O Lord, think of me, and take not revenge of my sins, neither remember my offences, nor those of my parents.

11. I said: O Lord, be Thou merciful to me: heal my soul, for I have sinned against Thee.

12. And now, O Lord, Thou art our Father, and we are clay: and Thou art our Maker, and we are the works of Thy hands. Be not very angry, O Lord, and remember no longer our iniquity: Behold, see we are all Thy people.

13. Lord, save us, we perish.

14. Lord, save me.

Prayers

As the child develops, the form of prayers he will learn will change. The form of morning prayer will undoubtedly change from the simplest form to the use of the liturgical prayers of the Church. This will be generally the development. There will be, of course, an increase in the number of prayers, so that by the end of the elementary school the student will be acquainted with the principal prayers of the Church.

1. Morning prayers
2. Evening prayers
3. Grace before meals
4. Grace after meals
5. Act of Contrition
6. Act of Faith
7. Act of Hope
8. Act of Charity
9. Stations of the Cross
10. The Gloria
11. Prayers of thanksgiving and praise from the Psalms
12. The Confiteor
13. Litany of the Saints
14. Prayer before a Crucifix
15. Praying the Mass with the Missal
16. Joyful Mysteries of the Rosary
17. Sorrowful Mysteries of the Rosary
18. Glorious Mysteries of the Rosary

To teach prayers adequately, the instructor should understand what is meant by mysticism, and its relation to theology and asceticism. For this purpose an excellent introduction is Fr. A. J. Francis Stanton's *Catholic Mysticism* (Herder). The bibliography is excellent.

Hymns

Hymns are an important factor in reënforcing the general religious instruction and training, valuable for their own content, and, if properly taught, add an element of joy in religious instruction that is quite important. The child should, at the end of instruction, know the great hymns of the Church. In the seventh grade preference should be given to the liturgical hymns.

For the seventh grade there is suggested the following to be sung within the voice range of the children:

1. As the Radiant Dawn is Stealing
2. Adeste Fideles
3. Hymn to the Sacred Heart
4. To Praise the Heart of Jesus
5. Fount of Graces, Hail to Thee
6. Memorare of St. Bernard
7. Ave Maria!
8. Hymn to the Heart of Mary
9. Virgin Mother
10. O Spouse of Mary
11. Memorare of St. Joseph
12. With Tender Love
13. Sweet Angel of Mercy
14. Hymn to the Holy Name
15. The Seven Gifts of the Holy Spirit
16. Upon the Altar Night and Day
17. Holy God, We Praise Thy Name

Liturgy

The pupils are by this time familiar with the Ordinary of the Mass, and should complete their memorizing it in these grades, including the Last Gospel. In this grade the attention of the children is called to the varying parts of the Mass which they follow in their Missal, and special study is made each week of the Mass of the Sunday and of the holydays of obligation. This will be done in preparation on the Friday of each week and on the vigil of the feasts of holydays of obligation. The essential text in this grade is the Missal itself for Sundays and holydays of obligation, and Fr. Cunningham's *Christ's Gift: the Mass*. This is the same text as is used in the sixth grade.

"The Character Calendar" in the CATHOLIC SCHOOL JOURNAL (September, 1930 to June, 1931) is suggestive of the applications of the liturgical facts to our personal life. Valuable as a further supplement to the main text of the grade, the Missal itself, would be *With Mother Church* (Liturgical Press, Collegeville, Minn.), Vol. III or IV or both. Volume III could be used in the seventh grade and Volume IV in the eighth. Valuable, also, for fact information is Fr. Dunney's *The Mass* (Macmillan Co.), and Fr. MacMahon's *Liturgical Catechism* (Gill & Son, Dublin), and *St. Andrew's Daily Missal* (Lohmann).

Religious Information

There are certain facts about religious persons, vestments, ceremonies, and institutions that as a part of their culture, as well as essential or at least supplementary to religious practice, need to be taught, and specific provision should be made for the instruction.

One is surprised often to find adults who do not know what INRI means, or *Alpha* and *Omega*, or even IHS, why the Mass is said in Latin, or who some prominent character in the Old or New Testament is. The teacher should use every opportunity to give such information whenever she discovers there is need for it. In this grade will be taught, in addition to what the teacher discovers to be the need of the pupil, the following:

The Organization of the Church

I. Personnel
   1. Pope
   2. The College of Cardinals
   3. Bishops and Archbishops
   4. Priesthood
   5. Religious Orders
      a) Teaching
      b) Hospital
      c) Others
II. Divisions
   1. Vatican City
   2. Dioceses and Archdioceses
   3. Provinces
   4. Parishes
III. How Religious Orders are Organized

Christian Symbolism

I. Grape and Wheat
II. The Four Evangelists
III. Fish, etc.
IV. Architectural Symbolism

A specially useful source of questions and answers for this part of the course on religious information is Father John F. Sullivan's *Externals of the Catholic Church, Her Government, Ceremonies, Festivals, Sacramentals and Devotions* (Kenedy), and Father Conway's *The Question Box*. The new *Catholic Dictionary* is especially useful. For reference the *Catholic Encyclopedia* is indispensable.

This heading is placed in the curriculum so that the

teacher will realize the relative importance of this informational background to the main purpose, and will not give it undue emphasis at the expense of weightier matters. Information should be given as information.

Religious Practice

A definite part of the program in every grade is to build up the practice of religion in every grade and have the development cumulative throughout the grades. Wherever teachers see opportunity to build up Catholic practice they should do so. Teachers must not confound the lessons that may be essential and the actual practice in the life of the child. The pupil should understand the importance of interior disposition.

In the assignment to grade the purpose is to provide a specific time to see that the practice is established and understood. In some cases the habit will have been established. The cumulative listing of these practices is to emphasize the fact that they are not taught or established once and you are through with them. The practice must continue to be stimulated until it is "securely rooted in the life of the individual." There should be emphasized in this grade:

1. Morning Prayer
2. Evening Prayer
3. Regular attendance at Mass on Sunday
4. Attendance at Mass on all holydays of obligation
5. Angelus
6. Bowing at the name of Jesus
7. Tipping hat or bowing as one passes a church

8. Tiping hat when one meets a priest or Sister or other religious
9. Monthly Communion or more frequently
10. Keeping spirit of Lent by sacrifice
11. Saying Stations of Cross
12. Practice of saying brief prayers, ejaculations, or aspirations in time of temptation
13. Prayer for our parents
14. Praying the Mass with Missal
15. Frequent attendance at Benediction of the Blessed Sacrament
16. Daily recitation of Rosary during May, and frequent recitation at other times
17. Keeping the fast days and days of abstinence emphasized

Practical Life

The translation of the religious knowledge, practice, and attitudes in the day-to-day life of the child must always be an objective in religious education. The elevation of the actual daily life of the individual to a supernatural plane will come about through the character of the individual's motivation. This must be a matter of development; the child must be taken, however, where he is. The lines of development are indicated but the more specific content is left for the experimentation of the first year. A teacher should always take advantage of any actual situation, and should always strive to meet difficulties which her children as a group are confronted with, no matter whether it is included in the course of study or not.

1. Do a good turn every day for the love of God.
   a) Daily examination of conscience at night.
   b) Daily specific review of day's thoughts, words, and deeds.
   c) Weekly complete examination of conscience for confession, or as a preparation for spiritual Communion.
   d) Daily expiation for the temporal punishment due to sin.
2. Cultivation of virtuous life.
3. Cultivation of school virtues.
4. Promotion of corporal and spiritual works of mercy.

Special attention is directed to the chapters on "The Christian Rule of Life" and "The Christian Daily Exercise" of the *Catechism of Christian Doctrine* approved by the Cardinal, Archbishops, and Bishops of England and Wales, and directed to be used in all dioceses.

Basal Text and Supplementary Material

The text for the seventh and eighth grades should aim to coördinate the instruction of the preceding grades. In the process of giving more definite order and sequence to the material the child has already covered, the questions and answers of the *Baltimore Catechism,* and the English text of Cardinal Gaspari's catechism when it is ready, will be used as the succinct summary. In this way the doctrinal summaries will find their proper place psychologically in the development of the instruction. An experimental text is being prepared, *The Highway to God* (Bruce), which will be tested under the actual conditions of classroom work, and revised as experience indicates the need and character of the revision.

RELIGION IN GRADE VIII

Main Interest: Christian Doctrine

IN the eighth year the emphasis becomes more definitely doctrinal than it has in any of the preceding years, though it is not solely doctrinal. The instruction definitely provides for the study and learning of the specific questions and answers of the *Baltimore Catechism*.

Outline of Main Topics

The topics of study included in the seventh and eighth year shall be a definite organization of the material that they have learned in the more concrete situation of the preceding grades. The work of these two grades is one continuous unit. The line of division will vary with the different classes. The work in the eighth grade will begin with a comprehensive review of the topics covered in the seventh grade. The development of topics will be orderly, each one growing out of the preceding ones, and all will be related to life. Such an orderly development is contained in the following outline:

1. The Roman Catholic Church
2. Grace
3. The Sacraments in General
4. Baptism
5. Confirmation
6. Eucharist

7. Penance
8. Extreme Unction
9. Holy Orders
10. Matrimony
11. Sacramentals
12. Prayer
13. The Commandments of the Church
14. The Saints
15. The Angels
16. Summary: The Creed

Scriptural Passages of Doctrinal Significance

There are certain passages of Scripture that have a doctrinal significance or are the bases of the Church's formulation of the doctrine. These passages, some of them learned in another grade, should now be reviewed and others added, and all memorized exactly. These passages should be placed in their context by the teacher both as a help to understanding and to memory. The following list is minimum:

"So also is the resurrection of the dead.

It is sown in corruption, it shall rise in incorruption,

It is sown in dishonor, it shall rise in glory,

It is sown in weakness, it shall rise in power,

It is sown a natural body, it shall rise a spiritual body" (I Cor. xv. 42–44).

"I say to thee: That thou art Peter; and upon this rock I will build My Church, and the gates of hell shall not prevail against it" (Matt. xvi. 18).

"One body and one Spirit; as you are called in one hope of your calling. One Lord, one faith, one baptism. One God and Father of all" (Eph. iv. 4–6).

"I will give to thee the keys of the Kingdom of Heaven. And whatsoever thou shalt bind upon earth, shall be bound also in Heaven: and whatsoever thou shalt loose on earth, it shall be loosed also in Heaven" (Matt. xvi. 19).

"As the Father hath sent Me, I also send you. When He had said this, He breathed on them, and He said to them: Receive ye the Holy Ghost: Whose sins you shall forgive, they are forgiven them; and whose sins you shall retain, they are retained" (John xx. 21–23).

"Is any man sick among you? Let him bring in the priests of the church, and let them pray over him, anointing him with oil in the Name of the Lord. And the prayer of faith shall save the sick man; and the Lord shall raise him up: and if he be in sins, they shall be forgiven him" (James v. 14, 15).

"What . . . God hath joined together, let no man put asunder" (Matt. xix. 6).

"When the Apostles, who were in Jerusalem, had heard that Samaria had received the Word of God, they sent unto them Peter and John. Who when they were come, prayed for them, that they might receive the Holy Ghost. For He was not yet come down upon any of them; but they were only baptized in the Name of the Lord Jesus. Then they laid their hands upon them and they received the Holy Ghost" (Acts viii. 14–17).

"Going therefore, teach ye all nations; baptizing them in the Name of the Father, and of the Son, and of the Holy Ghost" (Matt. xxviii. 19).

"Unless a man be born again of water and of the Holy Ghost, he cannot enter into the Kingdom of God" (John iii. 5).

"When, therefore, they had dined, Jesus saith to Simon Peter: Simon, son of John, lovest thou Me more than these? He saith to Him: Yea, Lord, Thou knowest that I love Thee. He saith to him: Feed My lambs. He saith to him again: Simon, son of John, lovest thou Me? He saith to Him: Yea, Lord, Thou knowest that I love Thee. He saith to him: Feed My lambs. He said to him the third time: Simon, son of John, lovest thou Me? Peter was grieved, because He had said to him the third time: Lovest thou Me? And he said to Him: Lord, Thou knowest all things: Thou knowest that I love Thee. He said to him: Feed My sheep" (John xxi. 15–17).

Practical Applications of Religion

Definite provision should be made that actual cases of life problems should be considered where there is no doubt about the application of the religious principle or doctrine. Some typical cases illustrating the Commandments of the Church and the sacraments are presented as samples:

1. Into what society does baptism admit one?
May one, after joining, leave it at will?
What are the conditions of active membership?

2. In a certain grade school which a few Protestant children attended, the teacher had been explaining the sacrament of baptism. At the noon recess, two of the girls had succeeded, as they said, "in baptizing" one of their Protestant friends despite her violent protests.
Had they succeeded? Discuss.

3. Mr. Karz had never been baptized. On his deathbed he called for a Catholic priest and begged to be instructed and baptized before his death. After a brief period of instruction, Mr. Karz received the sacrament of baptism. He died immediately thereafter.
What does the Church teach about the state of that man's soul?
Would it not be better for all people to wait until they were about to die for baptism? Explain.

4. Thomas Bailey was frequently taunted by his school fellows because he never failed to remove his hat when he passed a Catholic Church and because he not infrequently stepped inside the church and made a brief visit.
Discuss from Thomas' point of view and from his school fellows' point of view.

5. Dick Steven would very much like to begin the practice of receiving Holy Communion daily. However, he hesitates because of the many venial sins he commits day after day.

Should this deter Dick from receiving Holy Communion daily? Discuss. How can Dick greatly overcome these defects?

6. On a questionnaire of a certain men's college they were asked "to please state frankly your own experience with frequent Communion." Here are some of the frank statements:

"I seldom if ever commit a mortal sin on the days on which I receive Holy Communion. If I stay away from the Sacraments for several days I usually fall into many and grievous sins."

"When I am receiving frequently, I am a soldier; when I am not, I am a moral traitor."

"I cannot do without it now. I actually feel a physical difference when I neglect it for a morning."

"I have received so many favors and such consolation from the practice that I feel that the old saying is true 'God can get along without you, but you cannot get along without God.'"

For your own self, decide if this is your experience.

Do you go to Holy Communion as frequently as you should?

Would it not be possible for you to go to Holy Communion weekly? Daily?

7. Ned Black was caught in the act of stealing a large sum of money. He was arrested and sentenced. Ned was sorry he stole the money because he was caught.

Ned has contrition. Is this contrition satisfactory for the reception of the sacrament of penance? Why?

How must contrition be?

Why should contrition precede the confession of sins?

8. Regina Walton is dangerously ill. The attending physician has advised her parents to call the priest. They defer, however, because they fear to frighten her. They carefully avoid speaking of anything that may make her realize the seriousness of her illness.

Of what are the parents guilty?

When should one call a priest?

Some people have a false notion regarding the reception of Extreme Unction. They think that when one has received the sacrament of Extreme Unction he is sure to die.

What is the purpose of the sacrament?

9. Bernard Quinn went to church on Sunday morning with the intention of hearing Mass. He was out late the previous evening, and consequently, fell asleep soon after Mass had begun and did not wake up until the Communion of the Mass.

Did Bernard fulfill his obligation? Discuss.

Why does the Church exhort the faithful not to attend late Saturday night functions?

When may a person be excused from hearing Mass?

10. Mr. Kendall, a Catholic, was looking for employment in a large city. He did not have a penny left and was obliged to beg for food. On a Friday he was given a meat sandwich.

May Mr. Kendall eat the meat sandwich?

How would the situation differ if we were not in great need for food?

When you are traveling may you eat meat on Friday? Discuss.

11. John Cannon refuses to observe the fast and abstinence regulations during the Ember weeks because he claims that the Friday abstinence and and the Lenten fast are sufficient.

Why is John, nevertheless, guilty of sin?

Why have the Ember weeks been instituted?

At what time of the year do the Ember weeks occur?

12. After a good confession and before receiving Holy Communion, Jack smoked a cigarette. Mary chewed gum. Mr. Jenden took a headache tablet. Some snowflakes blew into Jane's mouth.

Discuss each one's case. May they receive?

How does the law of fast oblige the sick?

13. Donald Brunner, 21 years of age, has a permanent position, is drawing a good salary, and has no one to support but himself. He feels that he is not obliged to contribute to the Church because his parents are regular contributors.

Why is Donald obliged to contribute?

How could Donald be led to understand his duty?

14. One Sunday morning Betty's mother was ready to go to Mass, when she heard that a neighbor was seriously ill and needed help. Instead of going to church she went to help the neighbor. Did she do right?

15. Marie was out to a dance all Saturday night. She was

very tired on Sunday morning, but decided to go to Mass before returning home. She slept all during the services. Did she fulfill her obligation to hear a Mass?

16. There was no school on the Feast of Corpus Christi and John and William decided to go fishing. John thought that the feast was a holyday of obligation, but he did not attend Mass. Afterward he heard from William that he was not obliged to hear a Mass on that day, as it was not a holyday of obligation. John said he was glad to hear that, for now he did not commit a mortal sin by not attending Mass. William said it would be a sin for John anyway, because he had been under the impression that it was a sin when he decided to stay away. Who was right, and why?

17. Mr. Peale is a Catholic. He goes to Mass on All Saints' Day but refuses to let his servants go as they are being paid for their work. Has he a right to prevent them from hearing a Mass?

18. Mr. Mack works in an office and cannot get to Mass on the Feast of the Assumption unless he rises at 4:30. Is he obliged to hear Mass?

19. May you stay away from Mass on Sunday because you have a slight headache? a toothache? because you cannot find your Sunday hat?

20. A boy commits a sin which he has never committed before. He is thoroughly ashamed of himself, feels disgraced, is remorseful. He hesitates and delays going to confession.

Is his attitude in accord with Catholic doctrine?

In the light of his sin and his feeling discuss purpose of the sacrament of penance and the Holy Eucharist.

Religious Vocabulary

Many of the words listed for the seventh and eighth grades have been previously met and studied in their context in earlier grades. The words have been definitely associated with ideas, and have been given in connection with concrete situations or specific explanations. In these grades, in connection with the more formal teaching of doctrine and the more exact formulation of Christian doctrine, there should be a checkup of the religious vocabulary in connection with a more formal word study. The word should be studied whenever the first opportunity in these grades presents itself, wherever the word is assigned. A tentative listing of the words used in the formulation of Christian doctrine is given here.

condemned	sacramental	anoint
absolution	bishops	profess
consecration	infallibility	temptation
sacrifice	doctrine	fortitude
resignation	morals	deceits
marriage	apostolic	persecution
contract	immortal	providence
intention	retain	instituted
scapulars	godfather	confession
distraction	administer	offend
abstain	chrism	precepts
solemnize	balm	contrition
plenary	beatitude	motives
nuptial Mass	piety	grievous
confirmation	relish	temporal
disobedience	remit	conscience
holy orders	transubstantiation	devotion
sacrilege	Holy Communion	dispensers
imprint	examination	dissolved
purgatory	capital	religion
harborless	sovereign	profession
abstinence	occasions	Rosary
mortify	conceal	ransom
baptism	almsgiving	contribute
guardian angel	corporal works of	indulgence
penance	mercy	remission
abide	confessional	resurrection
eternal	desire	Eucharist
vicar	godmother	Extreme Unction

matrimony
disposition
ordained
fast
fourth degree
spiritual treasury

communion of
   saints
sanctifying grace
supernatural
salvation
sacraments
invisible

authority
indefectibility
faith
proclaims
Roman
resolution

Poems

The poems suggested for the eighth grade carrying along the fundamental idea of the curriculum and furnishing reënforcement for the central interest of this grade are:

Praise to the Holiest in the Height, Cardinal Newman
Michael, The Archangel, Katherine Tynan
Relics of Saints, John Henry Newman
The Confessional, Helen Parry Eden
Hark! Hark! My Soul, Rev. F. W. Faber
Saint Bernard's Hymn, St. Bernard of Clairvaux
Mother of the Sacred Heart, Henry Coyle
In a Convent Chapel, James Clarence Mangan
Trust in God, Father Faber
The String of the Rosary, Maurice Francis Egan
The Babe of Bethlehem, Condé Benoist Pallen
At Easter, Charles J. O'Malley
A Ballad of Trees and the Master, Sidney Lanier
He was the Word that Spake It, John Doone
On a Picture of Our Lady, Dante Gabriel Rossetti
Mary's Intercession
One Thing Alone, Dear Lord! I Dread, Rev. F. W. Faber
Give Me, O Lord, a Heart of Grace, Lady Gilbert
The Sisters, Eleanor C. Donnelly
On the Feast of the Assumption, Eleanor Downing
A Ditty of Creation, Enid Dinnis
Prayer for a Levite, Speer Strahan
Our Daily Bread, Adelaide Anne Procter
A Legend, Adelaide Anne Procter

The Newer Vainglory, Alice Meynell
The Nightingale, Gerald Griffin
Extreme Unction, Ernest Dowson
Benedicti Domini, Ernest Dowson
An Autumn Rose-Tree, Michael Earls, S.J.
After a Retreat, Robert Hugh Benson
The Heaviest Cross of All, Katherine Eleanor Conway
Maris Stella, Augusta Theodosia Drane
Come, Holy Ghost, Who Ever One, trans. Cardinal Newman
All Ye Who Seek a Comfort Sure, trans. Father Caswall

Additional poems should be used emphasizing the center of interest in the grade. Children should be encouraged to "learn by heart" as many poems as possible. All should be required to learn some: many of the poems should be left to the student's own taste.

The more difficult poems will be read to the class by the teacher;* some poems will be read for their general idea without detailed study, and some poems will be studied in detail. Poems dealing with the same subject in earlier grades should be recalled to mind after the first reading of new poems. The poems suggested above, with others, are included in *Religious Poems for Children (Junior-High Grades)* (Bruce).

Aspirations, Brief Prayers, and Meditations

As opportunity offers, the following aspirations or others will be taught. One might be selected and written on the board each month, calling attention to it as opportunity permits. The students might prepare aspirations of their own. The following aspirations are suggested:

---

*Francis Thompson's *"The Hound of Heaven."*

1. Eternal rest give to them, O Lord, and let perpetual light shine upon them.

2. My God, unite all minds in the truth and all hearts in charity.

3. O Sacrament most holy, O Sacrament divine, all praise and all thanksgiving be every moment Thine.

4. May the most just, most high, and most adorable will of God be in all things done, praised, and magnified for ever.

5. We Thy people, and the sheep of Thy pasture, will give thanks to Thee for ever. We will show forth Thy praise unto generation and generation.

6. O God, my God, to Thee do I watch at break of day. For Thee my soul hath thirsted: for Thee my flesh, O how many ways!

7. One thing I have asked of the Lord, this will I seek after: that I may dwell in the House of the Lord all the days of my life. That I may see the delight of the Lord, and may visit His Temple.

8. As the hart panteth after the fountains of water, so my soul panteth after Thee, O God. — My soul hath thirsted after the strong living God: when shall I come and appear before the Face of God?

9. If I have found favor in Thy sight, O Lord, show me Thy Face.

10. Inflame our hearts with the fire of the Holy Spirit that we may serve Thee with chaste bodies, and please Thee with clean hearts.

Prayers

As the child develops, the form of prayers he will learn will change. The form of morning prayer will undoubtedly change from the simplest form to the use of the liturgical prayers of the Church. This will be generally the development. There will be, of course, an increase in the number of prayers, so that by the end of the elementary school, the student will be acquainted with the principal prayers of the Church.

1. Morning prayers
2. Evening prayers
3. Grace before meals
4. Grace after meals
5. Act of Contrition
6. Act of Faith
7. Act of Hope
8. Act of Charity
9. Stations of the Cross
10. The Gloria
11. Prayers of thanksgiving and praise from the Psalms
12. The Confiteor
13. Litany of the Saints
14. Prayer before a crucifix
15. Praying the Mass with the Missal
16. Joyful Mysteries of the Rosary
17. Sorrowful Mysteries of the Rosary
18. Glorious Mysteries of the Rosary
19. Apostles' Creed

To teach prayers adequately, the instructors should understand what is meant by mysticism, and its relation to theology and asceticism. For this purpose an excellent introduction is Rev. A. J. Francis Stanton's *Catholic Mysticism* (Herder). The bibliography is excellent.

Hymns

Hymns are an important factor in reënforcing the general religious instruction and training, valuable for their own content, and, if properly taught, add an element of joy in religious instruction that is quite important. The child should, at the end of instruction, know the great hymns of the Church. In the eighth grade preference should be given to the liturgical hymns. For the eighth grade there is suggested the following to be sung within the voice range of the children:

1. Come, Holy Ghost
2. Hymn to the Sacred Heart
3. To Praise the Heart of Jesus
4. Fount of Graces, Hail to Thee
5. Memorare of St. Bernard
6. Ave Maria!
7. Hymn to the Heart of Mary
8. Virgin Mother
9. O Spouse of Mary
10. Memorare of St. Joseph
11. With Tender Love
12. Sweet Angel of Mercy
13. Hymn to the Holy Name
14. The Seven Gifts of the Holy Spirit
15. Ave Maris Stella
16. Stabat Mater

Hymns From the Breviary and Missal

The following hymns from the Psalter and the Proper of the Season should be studied first for their literary content and then should be sung:

Holy God, We Praise Thy Name—Father Walworth and Monsignor Henry

O Christ, Whose Glory Fills the Heaven — Ambrosian (trans. by John Julian)

O God, Whose Hand Hath Spread the Sky — probably Pope St. Gregory the Great, (trans. by J. M. Neale)

Hail, O Queen of Heaven, Enthroned — (trans. by Father Caswall)

Hail to the Queen Who Reigns Above — Hermann Contractus, (trans. from Primer)

Come, All Ye Faithful — (trans. by Canon Oakeley)

All Hail, Ye Little Martyr Flowers — Prudentius, (trans. by Athelstan Riley)

Jesus, the Very Thought of Thee — St. Bernard, (trans. Father Caswall)

At the Cross Her Station Keeping — Jacopone de Toli, O.F.M., (trans. Fr. Caswall)

All Glory, Laud, and Honor — Theodulf, Bishop of Orleans, (trans. by J. M. Neale)

O Trinity of Blessed Light — (trans. by J. M. Neale)

My God, I Love Thee — St. Francis Xavier, (trans. Father Caswall)

Sanctify Me Wholly, Soul of Christ Adored — (trans. by T. I. Ball)

All Ye Who Seek a Comfort Sure — (trans. by Father Caswall)

That Day of Wrath, That Dreadful Day — Sir Walter Scott

Liturgy

The pupils are by this time familiar with the Ordinary of the Mass, and should complete their memorizing it in these grades, including the Last Gospel. In this grade, as in the seventh grade, the attention of the children is called to the varying parts of the Mass which they follow in their Missal, and special study is made each week of the Mass of the Sunday and of the holydays of obligation. This will be done in preparation on the Friday of each week and on the vigil of the feasts of holydays of obligation. The essential text in this grade is the Missal itself for Sundays and holydays of obligation, and Fr. Cunningham's *Christ's Gift: the Mass*. This is the same text as is used in the sixth grade.

The Character Calendar in the CATHOLIC SCHOOL JOURNAL (September, 1930, to June, 1931) is suggestive of the applications of the liturgical facts to our personal life. Valuable as a further supplement to the main text of the grade, the Missal itself, would be *With Mother Church* (Liturgical Press, Collegeville, Minn.), Vol. III or IV or both. Volume III could be used in the seventh grade and Volume IV in the eighth. Valuable also for fact information is Fr. Dunney's *The Mass* (Macmillan Co.), and Fr. MacMahon's *Liturgical Catechism* (Gill & Son, Dublin), and *St. Andrew's Daily Missal* (Lohmann).

Religious Information

In the eighth grade, informational tests will be given with no idea of grading the children, but primarily to fill in gaps that may have been caused by absence, transfer, failure to teach them, or any other reasons. Suggestive series of questions are given in the syllabus.

The religious information taught in the earlier grades will frequently be used in this grade by the teacher to reënforce, supplement, or illustrate the Christian doctrine taught in this grade. A special obligation is on the teacher in this grade, not only in this connection, but generally, to integrate the intellectual organization of the whole curriculum, and to do everything in her power to translate it into a practical guide in life.

Religious Practice

A definite part of the program in every grade is to build up the practice of religion in every grade and have the development cumulative throughout the grades. Wherever teachers see opportunity to build up Catholic practice they should do so. Teachers must not confound the lessons that may be essential and the actual practice in the life of the child. The pupil should understand the importance of interior disposition.

In the assignment to grade, the purpose is to provide a specific time to see that the practice is established and understood. In some cases the habit will have been established. The cumulative listing of these practices is to emphasize the fact that they are not taught or established once and you are through with them. The practice must continue to be stimulated until it is "securely rooted in the life of the individual." There should be emphasized in this grade:

1. Morning Prayer
2. Evening Prayer
3. Regular attendance at Mass on Sundays
4. Attendance at Mass on all holydays of obligation
5. Angelus
6. Bowing at the name of Jesus
7. Tipping hat or bowing as one passes a church
8. Tipping hat when one meets a Priest or Sister or other religious
9. Monthly Communion or more frequently
10. Keeping spirit of Lent by sacrifice
11. Saying Stations of Cross
12. Practice of saying brief prayers, ejaculations, or aspirations in time of temptation
13. Prayer for our parents
14. Praying the Mass with Missal
15. Frequent attendance at Benediction of the Blessed Sacrament
16. Daily recitation of Rosary during May, and frequent recitation at other times
17. Keeping the fast days and days of abstinence emphasized
18. One retreat a year
19. Reading ten minutes every day from New Testament
20. Memento of the Living
21. Memento of the Dead

Practical Life

The translation of the religious knowledge, practice, and attitudes in the day-to-day life of the child must always be an objective in religious education. The elevation of the actual daily life of the individual to a supernatural plane will come about through the character of the individual's motivation. This must be a matter of development; the child must be taken, however, where he is. The lines of development are indicated but the more specific content is left for the experimentation of the first year. A teacher should always take advantage of any actual situation, and should always strive to meet difficulties which her children, as a group, are confronted with, no matter whether it is included in the course of study or not.

1. Do a good turn every day for the love of God.
   a) Daily examination of conscience at night.
   b) Daily specific review of day's thoughts, words, and deeds.
   c) Weekly complete examination of conscience for confession, or as a preparation for spiritual Communion.
   d) Daily expiation for the temporal punishment due to sin.
2. Cultivation of virtuous life.
3. Cultivation of school virtues.
4. Promotion of corporal and spiritual works of mercy.

Special attention is directed to the chapters on "The Christian Rule of Life" and "The Christian Daily Exercise" of the *Catechism of Christian Doctrine* approved by the Cardinal, Archbishops, and Bishops of England and Wales, and directed to be used in all their dioceses.

Study of the New Testament

To round out the study of religion in the eighth grade of the elementary school, an *appreciative reading* of the New Testament should be the culmination of the study. This will be concerned principally with the Gospels. The minimum study should be the Gospel of St. Matthew with references to the other Gospels, at least the synoptic Gospels and the Acts of the Apostles. The curriculum will therefore include:

1. Gospel according to St. Matthew
2. Gospel according to St. Mark
3. Gospel according to St. Luke
4. Gospel according to St. John
5. Acts of the Apostles

This simple reading of the Gospels is to emphasize the fundamental conception of the course. "Foundation can no man lay other than that which is laid, which is Christ Jesus." The study, it should be noted again, is appreciative, not theological, or dogmatic, or merely factual. It is to further stimulate the love of Christ and to confirm the personal attachment to Christ. Any text of the New Testament (preferably without notes) will serve for this study. Each child should have his own copy.

Basal Text and Supplementary Material

The text for the seventh and eighth grades should aim to coördinate the instruction of the preceding grades. In the process of giving more definite order and sequence to the material the child has already covered, the questions and answers of the *Baltimore*

Catechism, and the English text of Cardinal Gaspari's catechism when it is ready, will be used as the succinct summary. In this way the doctrinal summaries will find their proper place psychologically in the development of the instruction. An experimental text is being prepared, *The Highway to God* (Bruce), which will be tested under the actual conditions of classroom work, and revised as experience indicates the need and character of the revision.

THE HIGHWAY TO HEAVEN SERIES

Prepared in the Catechetical Institute of Marquette University
(In co-operation with a group of Priests and Sisters teaching in the elementary schools)

GRADE	TEXT	MANUAL CURRICULUM IN RELIGION *(1st to 8th Grade inclusive)*
1	**THE BOOK OF THE HOLY CHILD** By *Sister Mary Bartholomew, O.S.F.* 96 pages	First Grade Teachers Plan Book and Manual
2	**THE LIFE OF MY SAVIOR** By a School Sister of Notre Dame 196 pages	Second Grade Teachers Plan Book and Manual
3	**THE LIFE OF THE SOUL** Prepared in the Catechetical Institute of Marquette University *Edward A. Fitzpatrick, Ph.D.* Educational Director 144 pages	Third Grade Teachers Plan Book and Manual
4	**BEFORE CHRIST CAME** By a School Sister of Notre Dame 256 pages	Fourth Grade Teachers Plan Book and Manual
5	**THE VINE AND THE BRANCHES** By the *Rev. R. G. Bandas, Ph.D.Agg., S.T.D. et M.* and a School Sister of Notre Dame 320 pages	Fifth Grade Teachers Plan Book and Manual
6	**THE SMALL MISSAL**	Workbook for the Missal
7 & 8	**THE HIGHWAY TO GOD** Prepared in the Catechetical Institute of Marquette University *Edward A. Fitzpatrick, Ph.D.* Educational Director 420 pages	Practical Problems in Religion By the *Rev. R. G. Bandas, Ph.D.Agg., S.T.D. et M.* (Answers problems in text)

www.ingramcontent.com/pod-product-compliance
Lightning Source LLC
Chambersburg PA
CBHW060831050426
42453CB00008B/652